SOCIETY AND LEGAL CHANGE

SOCIETY AND LEGAL CHANGE

SECOND EDITION

ALAN WATSON

Foreword by
Paul Finkelman

TEMPLE UNIVERSITY PRESS

PHILADELPHIA

For Sarah Alexandra Jardine Watson

Temple University Press, Philadelphia 19122
Copyright © 2001 by Temple University
All rights reserved. Published 2001
Printed in the United States of America
First edition © 1977 by Scottish Academic Press Ltd. Published in Scotland

♾ The paper used in this publication meets the requirements of the
American National Standard for Information Sciences—
Permanence of Paper for Printed Library Materials, ANSI Z39.48-1984

Library of Congress Cataloging-in-Publication Data

Watson, Alan.
    Society and legal change / Alan Watson ; foreword by Paul Finkelman — 2nd ed.
    p. cm.
    Originally published: Edinburgh : Scottish Academic Press, 1977. With new
preface by the author.
    Includes bibliographical references and index.
    ISBN 1-56639-919-X (cloth : alk. paper)—ISBN 1-56639-920-3 (pbk : alk. paper)
    1. Sociological jurisprudence. 2. Law—Great Britain. 3. Roman law. I. Title.

K370 .W37 2001
340'.115—dc21

                                                              2001034072

CONTENTS

Foreword by Paul Finkelman   vii

Preface to the Second Edition   xiii

Preface   xviii

Abbreviations   xx

Chapter 1:   Introduction   1

Chapter 2:   Roman Law: the System of Contracts   12

Chapter 3:   Roman Law: *Patria Potestas*   23

Chapter 4:   Roman Law: Further Points   31

Chapter 5:   English Law: Real Property; Tenure and Registration   47

Chapter 6:   English Law: Libel and Slander   61

Chapter 7:   Wider Perspectives   76

Chapter 8:   Legal Scaffolding   87

Chapter 9:   Legal Transplants   98

Chapter 10:   Causes of Divergence   115

Chapter 11:   Some Conclusions   130

Chapter 12:   Study of Legal Development   140

Index   147

FOREWORD

Legal Change, Legal Transplants
and the Scholarship of Alan Watson

In 1977 Alan Watson, then a professor of Civil Law at the University of Edinburgh, published *Society and Legal Change,* which is now brought out in its first American edition. Since then Watson has become one of the world's foremost scholars of legal history. Much of his work has been in Roman law, where he is generally recognized as the leading expert in the English-speaking world. Similarly, his work on the law of slavery is especially valuable. His *Roman Slave Law* (1987) is the definitive work in the field. His masterful *Slave Law in the Americas* (1989) illustrates the range of his work, bringing together his work in Comparative Law, the law of slavery, and Roman law. In the last decade Watson has branched into the biblical context of law, with such books as *The Trial of Jesus* (1995).

Because *Society and Legal Change* was first published in Scotland, it is appropriate and useful that it is now published in the United States, where American legal scholars are more likely to have access to it. The book provides a theory for integrating comparative legal developments both into legal history and more generally into legal scholarship.

Watson's theories, laid out here, are remarkably simple. In his earlier book *Legal Transplants* (1974), Watson argued that Comparative Law was, in the end, the study of legal development, of patterns of legal change, and thus of the relationship of law and society. Watson argues that to uncover these factors we must concentrate on the development of law over a long period of time and in different societies. Such study illuminates the similarities and differences, the causes of legal growth. Watson argues that the relationship between law, society, history, and social change are invariably the result of borrowing, whether from one of these societies by another, or from a common source, or both.

In *Society and Legal Change,* Watson follows up on some of his earlier work on the spread of law from place to place. As he argues in Chapter 9, appropriately titled "Legal Transplants": "at most times, in most places, borrowing from a different jurisdiction has been the principal way in which law has developed" (p. 98). This is certainly true in the English world. British colonists brought English (and sometimes Scottish) law to America, where they imposed it on a landscape and emerging culture, sometimes successfully, sometimes not. More successfully, Americans from the eastern seaboard moved west, taking law and legal ideas with them. Kentucky's first Constitution looks much like Virginia's; Tennessee's Constitution mirrored North Carolina's. On the Pacific coast Constitutions resembled those of mid-western states. Similarly, it is possible to talk about an American law of slavery, because most of the states borrowed from each other as the institution of human bondage spread west. Similarly, as Watson's own work shows, the master class throughout the Americas borrowed Roman law concepts when constructing legal regimes to support slavery.

Sometimes of course the borrowing is less voluntary. When the United States purchased Louisiana from Napoleon, the Francophone settlers suddenly were forced to "borrow" such concepts as the jury trial from their new American overlords. But, as Watson shows, such forced change cut for and against French law: Napoleon's armies brought law and legal theory with them, as they spread over Europe. Similarly, at least at the level of Constitutional development, the Allied victory and American occupation of the defeated Axis powers in World War II brought new legal ideas to West Germany and Japan; so too did the Soviet occupation lead to legal imposition on East Germany and eastern Europe.

The most obvious examples of this kind of borrowing and transplantation come from Roman law. And here, of course, Watson has always been at his best. In *Slave Law in the Americas* he shows how Roman slave law was taken to the New World, where it sometimes worked, and sometimes did not. But, however appropriate it was, Roman slave law became the model for the law of slavery throughout Latin America, as well as in Louisiana. In *Society and Legal Change,* Watson shows us the Roman borrowing where we might expect it, noting, for example, that "the theory that the Holy Roman Empire was a continuation of ancient Rome would play a very important role in Germany, but the general high quality of Roman law, the accessibility of the legal materials in the *Corpus Juris Civilis,* and the richness of the materials within a reasonable compass were the final and vital determinants" (p. 99) in the spread of Roman law into the early German states.

But he also shows borrowing from Roman law where we might not expect it. What is fascinating about Watson is his ability to teach us about legal borrowing and Comparative Law even in the modern era. Thus, he tells us the story of *Pahad v. Director of Food Supplies and Distribution,* a South African case from 1949. This case involved commodities "frozen" by a war board, which were stolen before the war board could take actual possession of the goods. Who then, suffered the loss? The court turned to Roman law, which it distinguished from the Byzantine corruption of that law, to help settle this very modern issue. Borrowing, not only across borders, but also across many centuries, still exists.

Part of the richness of this book, and indeed of all of Watson's work, is a function of the breadth of his scholarship. He cites works in English, Italian, German, Dutch, Latin, and French. His cases are from England, Scotland, South Africa, California, and Ireland, among others. He goes from the latest law review article to the *Mishnah* and the Twelve Tables of Rome with the ease that most scholars read the morning paper. In essence, the scholarship is breath-taking. This is how Comparative Law was meant to be done.

While further elaborating his thesis on borrowing, *Society and Legal Change* takes off in important new directions as well. Watson looks at legal systems in tandem as he explores patterns of development. His conclusions are startling. He argues that even in the most innovative systems, the persons with the power to change the law often do not do so for centuries even when the law is dysfunctional and harms these leaders. This is the case even when the elite are well aware that change would be helpful. For instance, the English introduced land registration into Ireland in the seventeenth century, and into their American colonies. This was a positive innovation. But England itself rejected registration until 1925, and it was not until 1990, after this book was first published, that the system was fully in place. Watson's argument is that legal cultures resist many useful innovations, such as land registration, in part because of inertia and in part because of the desire of legal actors to avoid radical change. The insight here, from English law, can of course be applied to American law. One simple example explains this. The English settlers brought with them English procedure with its cumbersome and impossibly complex writ system. Americans kept this system going for over a century and a half after independence. Watson's work may provide a theory to answer the question, Why did the legal profession resist wholesale procedural change until the promulgation of the Federal Rules of Civil Procedure?

Watson's work, especially *Society and Legal Change,* challenges the foundations of the traditional sociology of law. Watson published *Society and Legal Change* at almost the same time as Morton J. Horwitz's pathbreaking work on American law, *The Transformation of American Law* (1977). The two books offer contrasting visions and understanding of law. Horwitz propounded a concept of "instrumentalism" to argue that judges, particularly American judges in the nineteenth century, consciously used their power to reshape the law in order to help some industries at the expense of others. The law and economics movement, which began to grow at about this time, had of course a similar thrust, but with a different conclusion. Where Horwitz saw special interests gaining power, the conservatives of the law and economics movement saw efficiencies where the law worked and developed "right," and inefficiencies where the law did not develop. From a slightly different perspective James Willard Hurst, the dean of American legal historians, argued two decades before, in *Law and the Conditions of Freedom in the Nineteenth Century United States* (1956) that law was the catalyst for the release of creative energies among settlers.

Watson offers two complimentary and equally compelling theories of legal development. The first, which is found throughout his work, is the notion of borrowing. In this sense, Watson dovetails a bit with Hurst and also John Reid. Hurst's western settlers brought law with them, and used it to provide the mechanisms for economic development. This is a kind of borrowing. John Reid, in *The Law for the Elephant: Property and Social Behavior on the Overland Trail* (1997), described how settlers carried the law with them on the wagon trains. This too mirrors Watson's notions of borrowing. However, Watson takes the borrowing further, seeing it in global terms. Unlike most legal historians, Watson's work is not limited by time, geography, or language.

Watson's second theory, which is the major thrust of *Society and Legal Change,* differs from Horwitz, Hurst, and the law and economics scholars. Here Watson offers the suggestion, radical at least in 1977, that the legal system may not be so much about change as it is about continuity and repetition. This is implicit in the concept of legal transplantation and borrowing. Rarely, Watson argues, do judges and legislatures actually create new law; rather, they borrow from others or, as is often the case, they make do with what they have. Thus Americans borrowed the writ system, already obsolete and cumbersome, and suffered with this antique system for a century and a half.

Dovetailing with borrowing is Watson's startling argument that legal systems will tolerate great inefficiencies before accepting change. This cuts against both Horwitz and the law and economics movement. Consider, as Watson does, English land law: The system was notoriously inefficient and, quite frankly, stupid. The rules of land ownership grew up in feudal times. The rules were complex then, and got worse over time. By Blackstone's time the rules made no sense at all, but, as Watson reminds us, in the hands of an expert, they could be manipulated to "produce almost any result which an aristocratic landowner could wish" (p.48). As Watson notes, such manipulation was expensive, and while "it is true that the rich can afford to pay for the services of the best conveyancers" it is also true that "even the rich can hardly be expected to take pleasure in doing so" (p.48). Thus it would seem, from an instrumentalist perspective, like that of Horwitz, the land system should have been replaced by something less cumbersome and less expensive, but still supportive of the economic and social goals of the elite. From a law and economics perspective the system should also have changed, because it was simply inefficient and too expensive. Significantly, Horwitz sees some English innovations, like the fellow servant rule, as instrumentalist. If English judges were instrumentalist, or economically efficient, just as their American counterparts, they should have moved against the land system. But, as Watson notes, the system did not change. It instead went on and on and on with its costly conveyancers and dangerously complex rules. Thus, despite the "importance of real property in English law," the land law system remained "out of step with society" (p. 49).

Most legal historians, looking at one society, one country, and one time period, offer explanations about legal change. Watson's great contribution is that he offers us a theory of legal stagnation. He explains why law does not change, rather than telling us why it did change. This is a remarkable contribution, since so often law does not change.

Watson's insight into how law changes or remains the same is informed by his argument that the legal history of one country cannot be understood in isolation. Every legal historian, he implies, must be a comparativist, and conversely every comparative lawyer must be a historian. We can of course dispute the thesis. Many of us work in the legal history of one country and even in one slice of that country's history. Our work nevertheless can be fruitful and important. But surely, Watson's comparative insights can improve our understanding of what we do. Every legal historian cannot be a comparativist, but surely we can all learn from the kind of comparative legal history that Watson offers in this book. Furthermore, we can test our findings against Watson's theories. My guess is, that if we do, our work will be vastly improved.

Many scholars will continue to reject the idea of transplantation or borrowing; more will be uncomfortable with the idea that the legal system will tolerate inefficiency to avoid change. But whether we reject or accept either thesis, our work will be enriched by coming to terms with Watson's ideas and arguments.

Paul Finkelman
Chapman Distinguished Professor of Law
University of Tulsa College of Law

PREFACE TO THE SECOND EDITION

When Douglas Grant, publisher of the first edition, invited me to consider republication of this book I was delighted. Then I was surprised to find that I wished to make no changes. The message of the book remains as it was in 1977. But a short preface seems appropriate. My starting point is a recent comment by Charles Donahue with which I am partly in agreement. He writes:[1]

> Conscious or unconscious borrowing of institutions, ideas, ways of thought, or whole codes is a legitimate topic of comparative inquiry, but it is not in itself a topic of comparative inquiry. To say that Turkey adopted the Swiss Civil Code and Swiss Code of Obligations in 1926 is not a comparative statement; it is a statement about the history of Turkish law. To engage in comparative inquiry we must compare. We must, for example, show that the Swiss Civil Code was interpreted differently in Switzerland from the way it was interpreted in Turkey — or that it was interpreted in the same way. We must ask how adoption of the Swiss Civil Code impacted on Turkish society in comparison with how it impacted on Swiss society. We must ask what happened when a body of law that presupposes a whole series of western ideas about the nature of law and governance was adopted by a people that did not fully share those ideas.
>
> To say this, of course, is an implied criticism of one aspect of the work of the man who is probably the most prominent comparative legal historian in North America, Alan Watson. Watson's work is stimulating. There is no question that his numerous works on the history of the transplant and reception of legal rules have arrived at a comparative conclusion. To put it perhaps too bluntly, in Watson's view the legal profession in most western societies is so out of touch with reality that social forces have relatively little effect on the way that legal systems develop. That conclusion may be right. My problem with it is that by focusing almost exclusively on the formal statements of the rules rather than on their interpretation, their impact on society and their interaction with the high-level ideas that surround them, Watson has made it too easy for himself. He is doing comparative work, but it is comparative work that ignores some of the more important questions that the method inspires.[2]

This preface is particularly apt for commenting on the comment. Donahue is, of course, correct that my main focus in comparative legal history has been on the formal statements of the rules. But he misleads when he claims that this focus is almost exclusive. Indeed, specifically on the impact of the reception of Swiss law in Turkey I wrote: "Even after such legislation a reception is not a once and for all act, but a social process extending over many years. The result will not be Swiss law in Turkey, but Turkish law that owes much to Swiss legal culture, concepts and rules."[3] When one writes about legal borrowing the focus must be on rules, institutions, and structures. That is what is appropriated. One can borrow Roman legal rules but not the spirit of Roman law.[4] In the nature of things, legal rules that are identical whether as a result of borrowing or not will operate differently in two societies. The Dominican Republic took over the French *code civil* in 1845, even leaving it untranslated until 1884. No one (I imagine) would think that in 1860 the rules of contract operated in the same way in the two countries. Indeed, in my earliest sustained effort on comparative law I wrote:

> Variations in the political, moral, social and economic values which exist between any two societies make it hard to believe that many legal problems are the same for both except on a technical level. For instance, the legal problem of rent restriction is not the same both in a country where rented accommodation is common and in a country where it is less common; the problem of alimony for divorced wives in a jurisdiction where it is usual for women to work differs from that in a country where women do not have jobs;[5] that problem and the proper legal response to it may also be altered by the availability or otherwise of crèches and nursery schools for young children; the legal problem of the enforceability of contracts against minors will vary with the affluence of the society, the age at which young people become accustomed to living on credit, and the extent to which residing away from their parents is prevalent.[6]

Professor Donahue writes: "We must ask how adoption of the Swiss Civil Code impacted on Turkish society in comparison with how it impacted on Swiss society."[7] We may ask the question but it would be foolish to expect a satisfactory answer.[8] Comparative law and comparative legal history are in their infancy. Professor Donahue's approach would subject them both to crib-death syndrome. We must begin with simple questions: on the nature of the borrowing of legal rules; on their how, when, and why. Actually the answers here are also not so simple. At the same time we may study the impact of one identical rule on similar persons in the two societies. But we cannot at this stage of the game evaluate the impact on a society as a whole of the acceptance even of a single rule, far less of a whole code.[9] The extent of the difficulty becomes plain when we notice that even within one country legal rules impact very differently on different groups.[10]

In *Society and Legal Change* I am dealing specifically with the impact of legal rules on society. In particular I look at the phenomenon of survival of legal rules long after it is well known that their effect is not beneficial.

My proposition of a high survival rate of known harmful legal rules in Western states can, I believe, be generalized, but for clarity and simplicity I concentrate on two restricted areas: the two most admired legal systems; and rules which are disadvantageous to the ruling elite or some powerful section of society. If Roman law and English law can support laws that are known to operate badly and unnecessarily so for the leaders of the society, then surely we may assume that other Western societies will long tolerate legal rules that impact badly on other societal groups?

Roman *patria potestas,* the power of a father over his children and grandchildren, meant above all that persons in paternal power could own no property. This was true no matter the age of the son, even if he were consul, the highest state official. *Patria potestas* could have little meaning for the poor, the bulk of the free Roman population, but would bear heavily on grown-up sons from the wealthy classes. But *patria potestas* did not disappear. Absence of registration of title to land and unnecessary complication of tenure in England long survived to the harm of the property-owning classes who controlled Parliament.[11] Well-known and attested absurdities in the law of libel long continued to the great disadvantage of wealthy and powerful newspaper proprietors.

This volume is one of an ongoing series of works in which I try to tease out and account for aspects of law and its relationship to the society in which it operates.[12] In the earliest of these, *Legal Transplants,* I seek to show the enormous extent of legal borrowings, and to indicate some of the implications. In *The Making of the Civil Law*[13] I try to bring out something of the importance of the legal tradition itself for the shaping of legal institutions and rules. In a book in progress, still untitled, I hope to show that the dominant characteristics of any particular legal system are the product of a small number of recognizable elements.

I should like to leave the last word of this preface to F. W. Maitland, probably the greatest of all English legal historians: "The law of Husband and Wife is in an awful mess (I don't think that a layman would really believe how bad it is). . . ."[14]

Since 1977 I have reflected often on the basic message of *Society and Legal Change:* that law that was prejudicial to the ruling elite who had power to change it could long remain in force. A paradox. But I have not written to the point. Rather I have been much occupied with related issues: patterns of legal development in systems where the input of society is in the background. How can it be that very different social systems undergo similar legal growths? How can governments for so much of the time be indifferent to private law? Why, when great legislators appear, such as Justinian, Frederick the Great, Napoleon, Atatürk, is there so little of a precise social or economic message in their law? In the hope that this new edition will provoke controversy, I append a chronological list of my subsequent works that may be useful.

Books

The Making of the Civil Law (Cambridge, MA, Harvard University Press, 1981).
The Sources of Law, Legal Change and Ambiguity (Philadelphia, University of Pennsylvania Press, 1984; European edition, Edinburgh, T. & T. Clark, 1985; 2d ed. University of Pennsylvania Press, 1998).
Failures of the Legal Imagination (Philadelphia, University of Pennsylvania Press, 1988).
Studies in Roman Private Law (London, Hambledon Press, 1991).
Joseph Story and the Comity of Errors (a Case Study in Conflict of Laws) (Athens, University of Georgia Press, 1992).
Legal Transplants, 2nd ed. (Athens, University of Georgia Press, 1995).
Law Out of Context (Athens, University of Georgia Press, 2000).
The Evolution of Western Private Law (Baltimore, Johns Hopkins University Press, 2001).

Articles

'Comparative Law and Legal Change,' *Cambridge Law Journal* (1978), pp. 313–336.
'The Justice of the U.S. Constitution,' *International Journal of Moral and Social Studies* (1985), pp. 21–30.
'Slavery and the Development of Roman Private Law,' *Bullettino del Istituto di Diritto Romano* (1987), pp. 105–118.
'Chancellor Kent's Use of Foreign Law,' in *The Reception of Continental Ideas in the Common Law World, 1820–1920,* ed. by M. Reimann (Berlin, 1993), pp. 45–62.
'Thinking Property at Rome,' *Chicago-Kent Law Review* (1993) (Symposium on Slave Law), pp. 1355–1371. (Reprinted in *Slavery and the Law,* ed. by Paul Finkelman (1997), pp. 419–434.)
'Seventeenth-Century Jurists, Roman Law, and the Law of Slavery,' *Chicago-Kent Law Review* (1993) (Symposium on Slave Law), pp. 1343–1354. (Reprinted in *Slavery and the Law,* ed. by Paul Finkelman (1997), pp. 367–378.
'The Importance of Nutshells,' *American Journal of Comparative Law,* (1994), pp. 1–23.
'Aspects of Reception of Law,' *Am. Jnl. Comp. Law* (1996), pp. 335–351.
'Trade Secrets and Roman Law: the Myth Exploded,' *Tulane European and Civil Law Forum* (1996), pp. 19–29.
'Fox Hunting, Pheasant Shooting, and Comparative Law,' *Am. Jnl. Comp. Law* (2000), pp. 1–38 (with Khaled Abu El Fadl).

Notes

1. 'Comparative Legal History in North America,' 65 *Tijdschrift voor Rechtsgeschiedenis* (1997), pp. 1ff at pp. 14f. In the following quotation I omit Donahue's footnotes.
2. This is what my mother would have called 'a left-handed compliment' because Donahue includes in his opening paragraph, "As I understand the

term, comparative legal history hardly exists any place in the western world today."

3. 'The Evolution of Law: Continued,' 5 *Law and History Review* (1987), pp. 537ff. at p. 551. At this point I was following E. E. Hirsch, 'Die Einflusse und Wirkungen ausländischen Rechts auf das heutige Türkische Recht,' 116 *Zeitschrift für das gesamte Handelsrecht* (1954), pp. 201ff. at p. 206. I also commented, "Again, many rules will have a different societal value in the two countries" (*Continued,* p. 553).

4. Cf. already, Alan Watson, 'The Origins of the *Code Noir* Revisited,' 71 *Tulane Law Review* (1997), pp. 1041ff. at p. 1044.

5. And where they have social security as of right, and where they have not.

6. *Legal Transplants: an Approach to Comparative Law* (1st ed., Edinburgh, 1974; 2d ed., Athens, Ga., 1993), pp. 4ff.

7. 'Comparative Legal History,' p. 14.

8. I should perhaps make explicit some of my disagreements with the passage quoted from Professor Donahue. I emphatically oppose his view that drawing comparisons—usually a hopeless task—is central to Comparative Law: *Legal Transplants,* pp. 1ff., especially p. 4. Drawing such wide boundaries for the subject is a prime obstacle to making Comparative Law an academic discipline. That Turkey could receive Swiss law is equally emphatically for me a matter of Comparative Law, not just of Turkish legal history. What does it tell one about law in relation to society that there could be such a massive transplant (even though with different effects in Turkey from Switzerland)? His account of my view, beginning "To put it perhaps too bluntly," is too blunt.

9. One can, of course, study differences of interpretation of the identical rule by the courts of two countries.

10. This is the subject of Alan Watson, 'The Justice of the U.S. Constitution,' now in Alan Watson, *Legal Origins and Legal Change* (London, 1991), pp. 299ff. The complexities are enormous. For example, the U.S. Environmental Protection Act has many facets. To take one small example: what is the impact of the statute on human society when it is invoked with regard to the Spotted Owl in the Pacific Northwest? No generally acceptable answer will be found.

11. I need not say anything here of the absurdities of the Rule in Shelley's Case and the Rule against Perpetuities that survived so long in England to the harm of the landed gentry; but see A.W.B. Simpson, *Leading Cases in the Common Law* (Oxford, 1996), pp. 13ff., 76ff.

12. Richard Abel wrote a very critical review of the book when it was first published: 'Law as Lag: Inertia as a Social Theory of Law,' 80 *Michigan Law Review* (1982), pp. 785ff. For a response see William Ewald, 'Comparative Jurisprudence (II): The Logic of Legal Transplants,' 43 *American Journal of Comparative Law* (1995), pp. 489ff. at pp. 504ff.

13. (Cambridge, Mass., 1981).

14. Quoted by C.H.S. Fifoot, *Frederick William Maitland* (Cambridge, Mass., 1971), p. 53.

PREFACE

The argument of this book is that in the West rules of private law have been and are in large measure out of step with the needs and desires of society and even of its ruling élite; to an extent which renders implausible the existing theories of legal development and of the relationship between law and society. The ability and readiness of society to tolerate inappropriate private law is truly remarkable. The main but by no means sole cause of this divergence is inertia, a lack of serious interest in developing legal rules to a satisfactory point and in changing them when society changes. Theorists seeking to understand the nature of law have neglected the significance of inertia and the longevity of legal rules. Lawyers in fact have exaggerated the role of private law rules in promoting the well-being and happiness of society; society's essential stake in these rules is the avoidance or settlement of conflict, and for that their quality is of secondary importance. In the discussion the historical dimension of law is stressed. A legal rule has its being not only in the present but in the past, and the future develops from the present.

As always I have been lucky in my friends. Too many to be mentioned here discussed problems with me, but at one stage or another David Bentley, Prodromos Dagtoglou, Tony Honoré, Sandy McCall Smith, Neil MacCormick, and Gianfranco Poggi all read a draft to my great benefit. So did John Barton and Otto Kahn-Freund, both of whom went far beyond what could reasonably be expected from friends and colleagues in pointing out deficiencies and suggesting improvements.

A kind invitation from the Faculties of Arts, Law, and Social and Environmental Studies at the University of Liverpool to deliver six lectures on this subject in January and February, 1976 gave me a welcome opportunity to test reactions to my thesis. I could not here thank by name all those who provided stimulus, criticism and hospitality, but my gratitude extends to all individually.

As on previous occasions Mrs. Mary Schofield coped admirably with an untidy manuscript.

Finally, I must thank the Leverhulme Trust which allowed me to use the remainder of a research grant (awarded for a different purpose) to visit libraries to collect material and discuss points with European scholars.

Edinburgh   Alan Watson
April, 1976

ABBREVIATIONS

AJCL	*American Journal of Comparative Law.*
Bruns	C. G. Bruns, *Fontes Iuris Romani*, 7th edit. by O. Gradenwitz (Tübingen, Mohr, 1909).
Buckland, *Textbook*	W. W. Buckland, *A Textbook of Roman Law*, 3rd edit. revised by P. Stein (Cambridge, Cambridge University Press, 1963).
CLJ	*Cambridge Law Journal.*
Dicey, *Law and Public Opinion*	A. V. Dicey, *Law and Public Opinion in England During the Nineteenth Century*, 2nd edit. (London, Macmillan, 1914).
Farrar, *Law Reform*	J. H. Farrar, *Law Reform and the Law Commission* (London, Sweet & Maxwell, 1974).
ICLQ	*International and Comparative Law Quarterly.*
Jolowicz-Nicholas, *Introduction*	H. F. Jolowicz and B. Nicholas, *Historical Introduction to the Study of Roman Law*, 3rd edit. (Cambridge, Cambridge University Press, 1973).
Kaser, *RPR* 1	M. Kaser, *Das römische Privatrecht* 1, 2nd edit. (Munich, Beck, 1971).
Lawson, *Common Lawyer*	F. H. Lawson, *A Common Lawyer Looks at the Civil Law* (Ann Arbor, Univ. Michigan Law School, 1953).
LQR	*Law Quarterly Review.*
SALJ	*South African Law Journal.*
T.v.R.	*Tijdschrift voor Rechtsgeschiedenis.*
Watson	A. Watson.
Law Making	*Law Making in the Later Roman Republic* (Oxford, Clarendon Press, 1974).
Legal Transplants	*Legal Transplants, an Approach to Comparative Law* (Edinburgh, Scottish Academic Press; Charlottesville, University Press of Virginia, 1974).
Obligations	*The Law of Obligations in the Later Roman Republic* (Oxford, Clarendon Press, 1965).
Property	*The Law of Property in the Later Roman Republic* (Oxford, Clarendon Press, 1968).
Roman Private Law	*Roman Private Law around 200 B.C.* (Edinburgh, Edinburgh University Press, 1971).
Rome of the XII Tables	*Rome of the XII Tables: Persons and Property* (Princeton, Princeton University Press, 1975).
ZSS	*Zeitschrift der Savigny-Stiftung* (romanistische Abteilung).

Chapter 1

INTRODUCTION

Writers have long been fascinated by the relationship between law and society. As G. Sawer puts it:

> The material content of a legal system has always been seen to reflect in some sense the needs or demands of societies, whether of all societies or of a particular historically conditioned society or of a particular society considered as a type in a range of types.[1]

For many, law is intimately connected with the society in which it operates. For instance, among leaders of Western legal thought we have Montesquieu:

> The political and civil laws of each nation . . . must in fact be so particular to the people for whom they are made, that it is the merest chance if those of one nation can suit another.[2]

Or more romantically, Friedrich von Savigny:

> If we ask further for the subject in which and for which positive law has its existence, we find this is the people. Positive law lives in the common consciousness of the people, and therefore we have also to call it the law of the people (Volksrecht). But this should not be so understood as if it were the individual members of the people through whose arbitrary will the law is brought forth. . . . Rather it is the spirit of the people (Volksgeist), living and working in all the individuals together, which creates the positive law, which is therefore, not by accident but necessarily, one and the same law to the consciousness of each individual.[3]

The followers of this view are legion. Thus, Lord Cooper of Culross, a famous Scottish judge:

> The truth is that law is the reflection of the spirit of a people, and so long as the Scots are conscious that they are a people, they must preserve their law.[4]

E. N. van Kleffens:

> The history of a nation's law is a condensed history of its *mores*; it describes the unfolding of its concepts of what is permissible

and what is not, of what must be done and of what is merely recommended.[5]

And J. P. Reid:

Law is the signet of a people and a people are the product of a land. The primitive law of the eighteenth-century Cherokee nation reflects the mores, the integrality, and the rapport of the Cherokee people just as the characteristic traits of the Cherokees themselves reflect the physical environment of their existence: the mountains upon which they lived, the harvest reaped from forest, field, and stream, and the enemies – both in nature and mankind – that their geographical location required them to fight.[6]

A rather different, but equally significant view is maintained by those who believe that in early systems of law a common pattern of development is discernible. Credit for establishing this view must be given to Sir Henry Maine, and we may cite among more recent writers F. Pringsheim who declares:

A natural relationship exists at an early stage between all primitive legal systems; each system during its youth seems to pass through a similar process before the peculiarities of the nation are imposed upon its juridical order.[7]

A. S. Diamond opens his *Primitive Law Past and Present*[8] with the words:

The purpose of this book is to attempt an account of the general course of development of law from its beginnings until maturity.

Yet another opinion is that law is – 'is' not 'ought to be' – social engineering. Thus Roscoe Pound, who owes much to Rudolf von Ihering:

What then is the practical measure of values which the law has been using where theories have failed it? Put simply it has been and is to secure as much as possible of the scheme of interests as a whole as may be with the least friction and waste; to secure as much of the whole inventory of interests as may be with the least impairment of the inventory as a whole. No matter what theories of the end of law have prevailed, this is what the legal order has been doing, and as we look back we see has been doing remarkably well. . . . While philosophers are debating whether a scheme of values is possible, lawyers and courts have found a workable one which has proved as adequate to its tasks as any practical method is in any practical activity. Without putting it in that way they have treated the task of the legal order as an engineering task of achieving practical results with a minimum of friction and waste. ... I am not offering this idea of social engineering as a cure-all to be taken over by political and juristic theory and used to solve all the difficult problems of the science of law in the world of today. What I have set forth is no more than a description of how the legal order actually functions. It is a sketch of what courts do and jurists and judges have been doing since the Roman jurisconsults of the first century. In the whole development of modern law courts and lawmakers and law teachers, very likely with no clear theory of just what they were doing, have been at work finding practical adjustments and reconcilings, and if nothing more was possible, practical compromises of conflicting and overlapping interests.[9]

For still others, and not just Marxists, law is or represents the interests of the ruling classes. From Karl Marx himself – with Friedrich Engels – we have:

In actual history, those theoreticians who regarded *power* as the basis of law were in direct contradiction to those who looked on *will* as the basis of law. ... If power is taken as the basis of law, as Hobbes, etc. do, then law, statute, etc. are merely the symptom, the expression of *other* relations upon which the State power rests. The material life of individuals, which by no means depends merely on their 'will', their mode of production and form of intercourse, which mutually determine each other – this is the real basis of the State and remains so at all the stages at which division of labour and private property are still necessary, quite independently of the *will* of individuals. These actual relations are in no way created by the State power; on the contrary they are the power creating it. The individuals who rule in these conditions, besides having to constitute their power in the form of the *State*, have to give their will, which is determined by these definite conditions, a universal expression as the will of the State, as statute – an expression whose content is always determined by the relation of this class, as the civil and criminal law demonstrates in the clearest possible way. Just as the weight of their bodies does not depend on their idealistic will or on their arbitrary decision, so also the fact that they enforce their own will in the form of statute, and at the same time make it independent of the personal arbitrariness of each individual among them, does not depend on their idealistic will. Their personal rule must at the same time be constituted as average rule. Their personal power is based on conditions of life which as they develop are common to many individuals, and the continuance of which they, as ruling individuals, have to maintain against others and, at the same time, maintain that they hold good for all. The expression of this will, which is determined by their common interests, is statute. . . . The same applies to the classes which are ruled, whose will plays just as small a part in determining the existence of statute and the State.[10]

And there is the statement made by Tumanov:

We Marxists assert that law is carried out in practice by means of coercion and violence, because all law is a class law, and the law of the class without coercion is not a law.[11]

However different these views may be, their proponents – along with many other legal scholars – have in common the firm belief that legal development is very much a rational response or is *the* natural response to existing circumstances, social, economic, political, geographical and so on, including religion.[12] Law could not be 'the spirit of the people' unless it accurately reflected the needs and desires of the people. Law in early society could not everywhere have the same general pattern of development unless it were that such people everywhere, above all in underdeveloped economic circumstances, had to face similar problems and approached them in a manner conditioned by their circumstances, giving the best answer available to them. The legal order could not operate well as social engineering unless it were in tune with the needs and desires of the society. All law could not be class law unless the class in question recognised its interests (consciously or unconsciously) and protected them by coercion.

This fundamental assumption of rationality in legal development or of a response determined by the circumstances seems to me to be inadequate and falsifies the relationship between law and the society in which it operates. It has, however, enough truth in it to be superficially plausible. No reasonable person would want to deny that to some extent a people's law is peculiar to it, that the law does reflect that people's desires and needs. Everyone would accept that certain problems are common to many relatively simple societies, and that at times the responses of societies – which have no connection with one another – are similar. It is easy to agree that a legal rule is often the result of social engineering especially if we consider only case law, or a statute when it is passed. And who would deny that much of law reflects the interests of the ruling élite? Moreover, pointing to occasional blemishes or lapses from rationality or circumstanced causality in systems would not greatly affect these theories. Most scholars who hold any of the views expressed in the preceding paragraphs would concede that there were instances where the relationship was not perfect, whether because past history influenced the course of legal development, law lagged behind social changes, a mistake was made in choosing the best response, the power of the proletariat was growing, individual law-makers were careless, greedy or biased, and so forth. The idea of a lapse from a perfect relationship between law and society can also, as we shall see in a moment, be expressly built into any of these theories. Moreover, many scholars bring the idea of a 'time-lag' into their discussion of legal development.[13]

Yet even if one accepts that some plausibility or truth is contained in each or any of these theories and one also allows for the obvious qualification of occasional lapses and a time-lag, each theory based on the idea of rational legal development or of law naturally responding to circumstances seems to me unsatisfactory. None of them pays or can pay sufficient attention to the numerous factors which cause law to be out of step with its society.

It is the thesis to be maintained in this book that, though there is a historical reason for every legal development, yet to a considerable extent law in most places at most times does not progress in a rational or responsive way, and that the divergence between law and the needs or wishes of the people involved or the will of the leaders of the people is marked. There is a divergence in the sense in which I am using the term when the legal rule, principle or institution is inefficient for its purpose in satisfying the needs of the people or the will of its leaders and when a better rule could be devised, *and* where both the inefficiency and the possibility of marked improvement are known to the persons concerned. Divergences appear in many shapes and sizes and might be classified in various ways whether in terms of how they come into existence or the effect they have upon the legal system or upon society in general. The main causes of divergence will be discussed in chapter ten after we have examined instances of actual divergence; and the complication which divergences bring to the legal system is the subject of chapter eight. As for their effect upon society in general this is basically either to produce a result different from what society could wish or need or, whatever the end result, to increase unnecessarily the economic costs. Further classification of legal divergences is not here necessary.

Rules of law which produce results which are intolerable to the society or its ruling class will no doubt be replaced. But to argue that in consequence any given system of law will reflect the needs and desires of society or its ruling class is a *non sequitur* unless we take that proposition in a very restricted sense indeed. Society and ruling classes are, in practice, able to tolerate a great deal of private law which serves neither the interests of society at large or its ruling class nor the interests of anyone else.

To prove this thesis one should ideally look at every aspect of law and legal development in every system, past and present. In practice this approach is as out of the question here as it is for any of the 'rational or causal theories' of law and society. Yet obviously it is not sufficient to examine at random a few instances in several systems where law and society are out of step. What can be done is to look at the pattern of growth in important areas of law in some of the major systems, and also to examine closely some of the details which can be regarded as most important for the society's outlook. I shall restrict myself to developed Western law.[14] If we find it reasonably easy to spot in Roman law, in English law, in systems deriving from these, major instances where law and the wishes or needs of the society or its leaders are not greatly in harmony then I believe the thesis may be regarded as proved. Codification introduces new complicating factors without, however, greatly disturbing the over-all picture. At an appropriate point I will explain why in the present work I am leaving modern codified systems aside.

The closeness of the relationship between law and society will vary from one branch of law to another. It should be stressed that in this work I will consider only the subjects traditionally considered as private law; not administrative or constitutional law, not social welfare law, not criminal law except that with regard to this last I will permit myself occasional lapses.[15] What I want to do is say something about private law, and the conclusions will be restricted to that. It may be, but need not be, that the great divergence which I think exists between private law and the needs of the society has parallels in other areas of law, and I will produce a few examples especially from criminal law to indicate the possibility of some divergence. But this is a book about private law and society.

As I mentioned in passing, some theories have expressly built into their views an inevitable degree of divergence between law and society at large. For instance, it was an essential part of Savigny's case that statutory intervention for a higher political purpose could easily be a fruitless corruption of law.[16] Again Marxists, especially Friedrich Engels, have argued that when the new division of labour makes professional lawyers necessary, then this new independent sphere of law, which is generally dependent on production and trade, has also a special capacity for reacting upon these spheres. In a modern state Engels claims:

> Law must not only correspond to the general economic condition and be its expression, but must also be an *internally coherent* expression which does not, owing to inner contradictions, reduce itself to nought. And in order to achieve this, the faithful reflection of economic conditions suffers increasingly.[17]

A different point of view often finds expression especially among anthropologists. Thus, Paul Bohannan:

> Law is never a mere reflection of custom, however. Rather, law is always out of phase with society, specifically because of the duality of the statement and restatement of rights. Indeed, the more highly developed the legal institutions, the greater the lack of phase, which not only results from the constant reorientation of the primary institutions, but also is magnified by the very dynamic of the legal institutions themselves.[18]

But I believe and hope to show that the divergence between law and society is far greater than those writers here suggest. When major weaknesses which are known to exist continue for centuries this cannot simply be the consequence of the duality of the statement and restatement of rights.[19] Nor can it be explained as a time-lag. If the concept of a time-lag has any real meaning it must be that when society changes legal rules do respond to the factors causing the change and to the new look of society, but some relatively short time elapses before law catches up (by which time society may have changed again). And many of the divergences of law from economic conditions cannot be explained by assuming a striving for an internally coherent expression of law. The instances discussed in the next chapter, on the Roman law of contract, will make this plain; indeed, in some cases a striving for internal consistency would have brought the law closer to economic conditions. The same chapter will also show that when a divergence between law and society occurs the reason is often not to be found, as Savigny claimed, in statutory intervention.

Let me sum up my thesis. All legal rules are created by a cause. The cause of their creation is commonly but not always rooted in social, economic or political factors important to the life of the society or its leaders. Likewise reasons can be given for the continuance of existence of legal rules. The reasons for their continued existence are, I believe, often factors which have no direct importance for the life of the society or its leaders. Often, indeed, the rules of law are in conflict with the best interests and desires both of the ordinary citizens and the ruling élite. Legal rules, once created, live on. They are frequently remote from the experience and understanding of non-lawyers, and are kept in existence by factors such as the absence of effective machinery for radical change, by indifference, by juristic fascination with technicalities, and by lawyers' self-interest.[20]

One of the most striking features of legal rules is their power of survival. Many, many rules endure for centuries with only minor modifications, both in their own land and abroad. The effect of this for the relationship between law and society is grossly underestimated. Theories of law and society, and of legal development, tend to focus on important innovations. This leads to the impression of a very close inherent relationship between law and the society in which it operates. If one looked more at the continuing life of legal rules a different picture would appear. The aim of the present book is to show that the relationship between rules of private law and society is much less close and inevitable than is envisaged by legal theorists. Although I wish to show that divergences occur for a variety of reasons my main desire is to make a plea for a redistribution of emphasis. The dynamic causal relationship between legal rules at any one time and the society in which they operate – whether this relationship is seen in Savignian, Marxist or Ihering-Pound terms – should be given less stress and the elements of inaction, above all the force of inertia, should be upgraded.[21]

Finally in this chapter one methodological difficulty should be made express. When one claims that law is in harmony or to a considerable extent is out of harmony, with its society or with a particular class in society, the impression may be created in the reader that one is treating the society or the class within the society as monolithic. Some legal theorists, as is well-known, have indeed maintained that what is good for the society or the class is good for each individual member of the society or class. Such a view, where it is held, makes the approach to the present thesis easier and hence need not be further discussed. Unfortunately I do not share it. The interests (and wishes) of an individual are, I believe, often at variance both with those of his society as a whole and with his class. This seems to me to be so not just in particular situations of conflict but often in general. Moreover, the interests or wishes of a group may be very different from those of the society as a whole, or of the class to which the individual members of the group belong. Or the groups with conflicting interests may be rather evenly balanced within the society. Rules may suit one class or one group which is very active in preserving them. It might be suggested that the result in a society will be a mixture of some rules which harmonise with the wishes and needs of the whole society or the ruling class and of others which suit particular groups or classes, and that when all the rules are taken together they form a pattern in which the various interests of groups and individuals are represented according to their strength in the society.

Thus it may appear ingenuous (or even disingenuous) of me to claim that legal rules are often out of step with the needs or desires of society. There may be various ways, some more theoretically satisfying than others, of coping with the methodological difficulty, but I hope (and believe) that the way I have chosen will be acceptable. The examples I will use to illustrate my thesis will, as far as possible, be cases where the dissonance between law and society cannot be seen as the result of continuing conflicting views where the legal rule which was in force was actively wanted and fought for by either a substantial minority of the population or by a significant number of those who held the political power. In other words, I will look for examples where the law actively benefits no recognisable group or class within the society (except possibly lawyers who benefit from confusion) and is generally inconvenient or positively harmful either to society as a whole or to large or powerful groups within the society. Whether the illustrations are successfully chosen for this purpose will be for the reader to decide at the appropriate point. But one advantage of this way of proceeding is that we need not concern ourselves with the definition of such sociological concepts as stratification, class, power.

It might also be argued that law is an institution of its society, exists in society, is part of society, hence cannot be said to be out of step with its society. The argument is no doubt correct in one sense, but is not in opposition to my thesis. To avoid being exposed to the argument I should perhaps say, that in general I use the word 'society' as a shorthand way of describing the people inhabiting a particular territory, or the citizens of a particular state.

Notes

1. *Law in Society* (Oxford, Clarendon Press, 1965), p. 147.
2. *De l'Esprit des Lois* (first published in 1748) book 1, chapter 3.
3. *System des heutigen römischen Rechts* 1 (Berlin, Veit, 1840), p. 14.
4. 'The Scottish Legal Tradition', in *Selected Papers, 1922–54* (Edinburgh, Oliver & Boyd, 1957), pp. 172ff at p. 199.

5. *Hispanic Law until the End of the Middle Ages* (Edinburgh, Edinburgh University Press, 1968), p. 28.

6. *A Law of Blood, the Primitive Law of the Cherokee Nation* (New York, New York Univerity Press, 1970), p. 3. Yet at p. 68 he says, 'But politics and law are not always reflected in social and physical conditions, . . .'

7. 'The Inner Relationship between English and Roman Law', now in *Gesammelte Schriften* 1 (Heidelberg, Winter, 1961), pp. 76ff at p. 76.

8. (London, Methuen, 1971), p. 3. For disagreement with the views reported in this paragraph see already Watson, *Legal Transplants*, pp. 12ff. Little emphasis will be placed on this theory here since we will be concerned with mature systems only.

9. *Contemporary Juristic Theory* (Claremont, Calif., Pomona College, Scripps College, Claremont Colleges, 1940), pp. 75f, 79ff.

10. From *Die Deutsche Ideologie* book 3. [In the Cotta-Verlag edition of *Karl-Marx-Ausgabe, Werke, Schriften*, it appears in *Frühe Schriften* 2 (Stuttgart, 1971), pp. 392f. It is conveniently reproduced in *Karl Marx, Economy, Class and Social Revolution* (London, Michael Joseph, 1971), pp, 270f. The present text is a modified version of the translation in that book. See also Marx's Preface to a *Contribution to the Critique of Political Economy* [reproduced in e.g., Marx, Engels, *Selected Works* (London, Lawrence & Wishart, 1968), pp. 180ff. Cf. M. Cain, 'The Main Themes of Marx' and Engels' Sociology of Law', *British Journal of Law and Society* 1 (1974), pp. 136ff.

11. Made at the Georgian Conference on Law (1930) quoted by D. Lloyd, *Introduction to Jurisprudence* 3rd edit. (London, Stevens, 1972), p. 670.

12. Law in certain fields may be regarded as reflecting religious beliefs rather than the desires or needs – other than psychical needs – of a people.

13. See, e.g. K. N. Llewellyn, *Jurisprudence, Realism in Theory and Practice* (University of Chicago Press, 1962), p. 55; O. Kahn-Freund, 'English Law and American Law – Some Comparative Reflections', *Essays in Honor of Roscoe Pound* edit. by R. A. Newman (Indianapolis, Bobbs-Merrill, 1962), pp. 362ff.

14. Hence, only to a very limited extent will we be concerned with the views of scholars such as Maine or Diamond.

15. Frederick the Great claimed that civil laws, as distinct from administrative and criminal laws, differ most from place to place: 'Dissertation sur les raisons d'établir ou d'abroger les lois', in *Oeuvres* 9 (Berlin, Decker, 1848), pp. 23f.

16. *Vom Beruf unsrer Zeit für Gesetzgebung und Rechtswissenschaft* 3rd edit. (Heidelberg, Mohr, 1840), p. 10. For H. Lévy-Bruhl, Savigny is right and law issues from the common consciousness, but statute (which is not essentially different from custom) is more supple than custom, and can adapt better to new conditions: *Sociologie du*

Droit 2nd edit. (Paris, Presses universitaires de France, 1964), pp. 55, 57.
17. Letter to C. Schmidt, dated October 27, 1890 (published in e.g. Marx, Engels, *Selected Works* (London, Lawrence & Wishart, 1968), pp. 684ff at pp. 686f.
18. In *International Encyclopedia of the Social Sciences* 9 (Macmillan, 1968), p. 76.
19. It should be mentioned that Bohannan's point is that this duality causes the law *always* to be out of phase with society. I believe he does not deny that the lack of phase may be greater.
20. Of course, the machinery for, and effectiveness of, legal change will vary from place to place and time to time. It will not be argued in this book that legal rules always remain equally distant from the needs and desires of society.
21. The theory of this book is in conflict with the words of L. M. Friedman, 'Some of the old is preserved among the mass of the new. But what is kept of old law is highly selective. Society in change may be slow, but it is ruthless. Neither evolution nor revolution is sentimental. Old rules of law and old legal institutions stay alive when they still have a purpose – or, at least, when they do not interfere with the demands of current life'; *History of American Law* (New York, Simon and Schuster, 1973), p. 14.

Chapter 2

ROMAN LAW:
THE SYSTEM OF CONTRACTS

The obvious starting place for such an investigation is Roman law which is not only the fountainhead of Western jurisprudence but has been and still is regarded as one of the finest creations of the human spirit.

It would be generally accepted that no part of Roman law has been so admired or so influential as the law of contracts. Yet that system of contracts had grave defects. It would, of course, be unfair to criticise the Romans for not developing contracts to the point that we have, or, with hindsight, to judge them for not producing a general theory of contract. But we can properly criticise them for major defects which lasted for centuries and of which they were aware or at least ought to have been aware.

The oldest Roman contract is the *stipulatio* which existed as early as the Twelve Tables, the codification of the mid-fifth century B.C. It can be regarded as the basic contract and in many ways is very satisfactory because it could be used for any lawful transaction and was very simple. It was a unilateral formal contract of strict law (*stricti iuris*) but the formalities were far from complicated. The parties had to be face to face, the promisee orally asked the promisor if he promised to give or do whatever it might have been, and the promisor promised using the same verb. Originally only one verb could be used, 'Spondesne ...?', 'Spondeo', but in course of time other verbs became allowable. The substance of the answer had to correspond exactly to that of the question.[1]

Formalities for making a contract have two evidentiary functions. First, they demonstrate to the parties involved that negotiations have come to an end, that the parties are now agreed and are at the stage of committing themselves. Secondly they are evidence that a contract was made, and in the event of a dispute provide proof both of the existence of the contract and of its terms. This second function is by far the more important. Yet the formalities for *stipulatio* perform only the first function and not also the second.[2]

This grave weakness of the *stipulatio* was well-known to the Romans yet was never directly remedied. To provide evidence it became common either to make the *stipulatio* in front of witnesses or to record the *stipulatio* in a written document. So usual did the latter course become that modern scholars discuss whether from the third century A.D. onwards the *stipulatio* had become a written contract.[3] It might be suggested that this lack of evidence in the *stipulatio* was in fact rather convenient since the stipulation could then be proved in more than one way. But apart from the fact that it is bizarre to have requirements of form which are absolutely essential for the validity of the contract but in themselves do nothing to prove the contract was made, we can be sure that the situation caused difficulties. Only too often would individuals make a *stipulatio*, content with the formalities of the contract, innocent of or indifferent to the difficulties of proof. The difficulties arising for a transaction when there was neither witnesses nor writing are well brought out by Aulus Gellius, *Noctes Atticae* 14.2, who refers not only to his own time, the second century A.D., but also to Cato the Censor who was active from the late third century B.C.

The form of the *stipulatio* with its built-in limitation is probably to be explained by its origins. In my view the *stipulatio* is likely to have arisen in circumstances in which the defect would not be apparent. Unfortunately the early history of *stipulatio* is very obscure and cannot easily be uncovered, and it would be wrong in this book to maintain one theory as opposed to another. But it should be stressed that the two theories which are most widely held support this idea. Thus, according to many scholars, the use of the verb *spondere* which is etymologically connected with the Greek σπένδω, 'I make a drink offering', points to a sacred background which involved the swearing of an oath.[4] Since a Roman oath was the calling of a god to witness and was not actionable before any tribunal, sacred or civil,[5] human witnesses would have no legal role to fill. The other major theory sees the beginnings of the contract in guarantees given in court proceedings by sureties who were named *praedes* and *vades*.[6] Since these guarantees would inevitably be made publicly, in front of a Roman magistrate, it is understandable that no specific requirements of witnesses developed.

A second major form of contract, the literal contract, which was constituted by entries made in the creditor's account books suffered from exactly the same fault that the formalities needed to constitute the obligation were insufficient to prove it.[7] The debtor's consent was necessary for the creation of the contract but the creditor's entries were not proof, and external evidence of this consent was needed. Little can be said about the history of the literal contract but it certainly existed from at least the late second century B.C.[8] and was flourishing – despite its defect – when Herculaneum was destroyed by the eruption of Vesuvius in A.D. 79.[9]

At this point it is instructive to turn from the formal *stipulatio* and literal contract to the informal consensual contracts. The consensual contracts, which were valid simply because of the agreement of the parties, without any requirement of form, were one of the great Roman inventions. The only consensual contracts were sale, hire, partnership and mandate.

Of these sale, *emptio venditio*, was certainly the most important, and perhaps the oldest, and seems to have been in existence in the later third century B.C.[10] Of it, around A.D. 200 the jurist Paul could write:

> Sale is a contract of the *ius gentium* and is therefore concluded by agreement and can be made by messenger or letter, without the parties meeting.[11]

Alas, for centuries that had not been the situation in practice for important sales, and can hardly have been accurate even for Paul's own day. There was originally in the contract of sale no inherent warranty against eviction; the earliest evidence for built-in protection – and even then the measure is rather primitive – is for the jurist Neratius who flourished under Trajan.[12] Nor was the seller held to give an implied warranty that the thing was free from serious latent defect existing at the time of the sale. Admittedly, from an early date inroads into the seller's freedom from automatic liability were made by the Edict of the curule aediles when the sale was made in the market-place or street and concerned a slave or beast of burden.[13] But although some steps may have been taken by the jurists to make such automatic liability more general this process seems still to have been in its infancy in the classical period.[14] Yet in most sales where the thing sold was of some value, the buyer would want to be protected against eviction and against latent defects. How could he achieve this? Answer: by taking stipulations. Hundreds of texts show that this was commonly done and was indeed standard. But then in practice a sale transaction would cease to have the advantages of a consensual contract in its formation. The parties would need to be face-to-face and make oral question and answer. The sale would then not 'be made by messenger or letter, without the parties meeting'.

Since the buyer so clearly wanted to be guaranteed against eviction and latent defects and the contract of sale did not automatically provide these guarantees, we must ask whether the concept of inherent warranties was too refined or advanced for the Romans in the early centuries of *emptio venditio*?[15] The straight answer is No! The ceremony of *mancipatio*[16] which was the main method of transferring the important things called *res mancipi* did contain an inherent warranty against eviction, which gave rise to an action for double the price stated in the *mancipatio*. And the aedilician Edict in effect provided an inherent warranty against latent defects; the seller had to declare physical defects and certain other faults, and if he failed to do so or if the health etc. of the slave or beast of burden was contrary to the declaration the buyer had right to an action. But, be it noted, the ceremony of *mancipatio* required the presence of the parties (plus others), and the wording of the aedilician Edict shows that it was expected that the buyer and seller be present together. It might be argued that the absence of implied warranties benefited the seller. But there is no social class of seller and no social class of buyer. In fact the impossibility of creating warranties other than by stipulation could make it more difficult for a seller to get a reasonable price for his goods. Where a stipulation could not be taken a merchant might well hesitate to buy at a distance.

The failure to have inherent warranties in *emptio venditio* from the beginning and for so long thereafter is a gross instance of law being out of harmony with society. Though express guarantees could be taken, these required the presence of the parties and cut down many of the advantages of the contract. This state of affairs is best explained, it seems to me, on the hypothesis that *emptio venditio* developed in circumstances where the defects would not be noticeable. I have argued elsewhere[17] that before the contract of *emptio venditio* existed, parties in an important sale situation would take *stipulationes* from each other. It would be difficult to make the *stipulationes* fully reciprocal or provide for all contingencies (since the *stipulationes* were contracts of strict law), and *emptio venditio* arose, I argued, to fill the interstices. Eventually *emptio venditio* was held to exist – or perhaps better actions *ex empto* and *ex vendito* would be given – in a sale situation whenever at least one *stipulatio* had been given, and the one constant *stipulatio* would be that against eviction and latent defects, since only that one would be needed in the simplest situation where the price was paid and the thing was delivered at once. When, finally, *emptio venditio* attained independent status as a contract, the actions given on it did not extend to the field of these guarantees – a *stipulatio* was still expected.

The remaining major class of Roman contracts is of those which are created *re*, by delivery. Of these *depositum*, deposit, need never have existed. It is the handing over of a moveable for gratuitous safekeeping, and the thing normally had to be returned on demand.

Why ever should it have come into existence after the introduction of the contract of *mandatum*, mandate, which was the gratuitous undertaking to do something – not necessarily to enter into contractual relations – for another? *Mandatum* existed by 123 B.C. at the latest.[18] The praetorian edict for *depositum* can scarcely be earlier than 100 B.C.,[19] and the civil law contract of deposit does not seem to be earlier than the late Republic – for which there is no evidence – or the early Empire.[20]

It is, of course, true that under the edict a depositee who failed to restore property entrusted to him following a riot, fire, house falling down or shipwreck was liable to pay double but this fact by itself does not justify the existence of a contract of *depositum*. The object could have been achieved by a less extensive edict, and *mandatum* could in all other circumstances have governed the gratuitous safe-keeping of another's moveables. This, however, is to reckon without the force of history. The XII Tables had established an action on account of deposit for double damages,[21] an action which must be regarded as based on delict rather than contract.[22] The edict which in effect created the contract of deposit was reducing the liability of the wrongdoing depositee to the depositor's loss except where the safekeeping had been undertaken in circumstances of particular stress to the depositor.[23] Of course, where the depositee's behaviour amounted to theft he would in any event be liable to pay double damages under the *actio furti*.

[It is instructive to glance at the Scottish Institutional writer, Lord Stair, whose celebrated *Institutions of the Law of Scotland* was first published in 1681. He declares (1.13.1):

Custody is called in the (civil) law *depositum* or *commendatum*, to which we have no suitable term in our law; but this contract is most fitly expressed by the duty and obligation thereof, which is 'to keep *and* preserve that which is given in custody', and it is here subjoined to mandate, because indeed it is a kind of it. For the lawyers do not so much notice the accuracy of logical divisions, whereby no member can comprehend another, as the usual terms known in law; and therefore they handle *mandatum, depositum et pignus*, severally, though all of them be truly mandates; and therefore *depositum* also may be fitly defined, to be 'a mandate or commission, given and undertaken, to keep and preserve something belonging to the mandator, or some third party'; and therefore, whatever hath been before said of mandates, must be here understood of custody, and needs not be repeated, except what is special in custody.]

The important distinction between the contract of mandate and the contract of deposit is, of course, that the former is consensual and needs only the agreement of the parties to come into existence, whereas the latter arises only when the thing is delivered to the depositee. It might be suggested that the reason for the Romans creating a specific contract of deposit lies here, that it was not thought right for a person who undertook to look after another's property to be bound before he took delivery. Such a suggestion would not be very plausible. To begin with, it is not immediately apparent that it is meaningful to draw a distinction here. If I ask you, and you agree, to purchase something on my behalf, then even if the purchase required no initiative but simply a visit to a shop, there is from the moment of our agreement a valid contract of mandate. Why should there be no contract if my request was to look after something for me, rather than to buy for me?[24] No satisfactory, logical answer can be given. In the second place, perhaps we cannot be sure that there was no contract arising from the agreement to look after the property. It is possible, though in the absence of texts we can say no more, that there was a contract of mandate.[25] Thirdly, although mandate was a consensual contract either party had the right, *re integra*, to revoke or renounce. Thus, if the contract of deposit had never existed and such a relationship had simply been governed by *mandatum*, no action would normally be available on *mandatum* until the thing had actually been handed over, just as was the case under the contract of *depositum*.

It should not be thought that the needless existence of an independent contract whose functions could have been performed by another is of little importance. Apart from the irrationality and the evidence of the absence of careful consideration of the needs of logical development, it is precisely factors such as the unnecessary proliferation of specific contracts which obscure the underlying common core and would make it more difficult to develop a general system of contract.

A further real contract, *mutuum*, merits discussion here. *Mutuum* was the only strict law (*stricti iuris*) real contract and it was the loan of fungibles for consumption. It was gratuitous, not in the sense that a counter-prestation made the contract void or turned it into something else, but in the sense that the action on *mutuum*, which was the *condictio*, would lie only for the value of the fungibles which had been delivered, and not also for any interest. When the lender wished interest he had to provide for it by taking a stipulation either for the payment of interest or for the return of the equivalent of the fungibles plus payment of interest. If the lender chose the first alternative, and the borrower defaulted, the lender would have to bring two separate actions, one on the *mutuum*, one on the *stipulatio*. This action on the *stipulatio* would also be a *condictio* if the rate of interest had been fixed. If the lender chose the latter alternative, he would sue only once, on the *stipulatio*. One can readily believe that in commerce *mutuum* as an independent contract was not prominent. As an independent contract it would not really meet the needs of the community, yet centuries passed without any basic alteration.[26]

The combined contract of *mutuum* and *stipulatio* is not neat, though we need not here go into the problems of theoretical classification.[27] But we should consider one practical problem. The action on a *mutuum* and that on a *stipulatio* of a certain sum of money or a particular thing (*certa pecunia* or *certa res*) was, as has been mentioned, the *condictio*. The statement of claim was in the clause known as the *intentio* and Gaius relates:

> 'A plaintiff who overclaims in his *intentio* fails in his case, in fact loses his right; nor is he restored by the praetor to his original position, except in certain cases in which . . .' – the rest of the text is lost.[28]

Let us imagine a case where a *mutuum* was made and a stipulation taken for the return of the equivalent plus interest, and a *condictio* was then brought which would, of course, set out the amount of the claim in the *intentio*. In practice the fact of the *mutuum* would be more easily proved than the taking of a *stipulatio*. Should the plaintiff not be able to prove that there had been a *stipulatio* then he would be regarded as having overclaimed in the *intentio* and his whole action would fail. He would not be allowed to recover the amount of the *mutuum*, and would have no right to bring any further action for it.

Until this point we have examined only recognised contracts. It was a weakness of Roman law that no general system of contract emerged but only individual contracts. For a contractual action to be given, the situation involved had to be within the sphere of a particular contract. We should not be too ready to blame the Romans for not making a development which we, with hindsight, can regard as logical and appropriate, but it may be reasonable to blame them for not recognising certain situations as giving rise to a contract. The most obvious and worst instance of a non-contract is barter.

The opening text of the Digest title on sale begins:[29]

> Sale originates in barter. For once there was no such thing as money, nor were there distinct terms for the merchandise and the

price but each according to his occasions and needs would exchange what was useless to him for what was useful, because it often happens that what one man has in superfluity another lacks.

It cannot be stressed too strongly that Paul here means that the factual sale situation developed from the factual barter situation, not that the contract of sale developed from the contract of barter. There was no contract of barter in any sense for centuries after the introduction of *emptio venditio*. The sole remedy available to someone who had handed over his goods and did not receive those agreed on in return was to bring a *condictio* for the value of what he had given. So unsatisfactory was this that one of the two great schools of jurists, the Sabinians, argued that for *emptio venditio* the price did not have to be in coined money, and hence that barter fell within the contract of sale. The opposing view of the Proculians prevailed, that the price had to be in money since otherwise one could not determine what was the thing sold and what was the price.[30] The significant thing for us is that the very fact that the Sabinians wanted to include barter within sale despite the obvious difficulties – and with a very far-fetched argument from Homer[31] – shows the jurists' awareness of how inadequate was the law on barter.

The steps in the development of actions against the non-performing party in barter are exceptionally obscure and much disputed,[32] but it has not been suggested that any action was available for the value of the counter-prestation before the early Empire. Indeed, most scholars would place any substantial development considerably later. We need not enter the controversy since it is enough for our purposes that in any event it took until the Empire for a remedy to emerge, and the Sabinians' views on barter as sale show that in their time barter was still not an adequately protected contract.

We have by now looked at fundamental aspects of the most important verbal contract, the sole literal contract, the most important consensual contract, two very different real contracts and a non-contract, and found grave defects where the needs and desires of the Roman people or its leaders were not met or not helped and where the development of rules, or lack of development, was not reasonable. The defects were not of short duration – it is not just a case of law reacting sluggishly – and in most cases Roman lawyers and men of affairs can be shown to have been aware of the defects. The Roman contractual system cannot be said to have developed in a straighforward way responding in a rational manner either to growing legal sophistication or to social needs. There is no close correlation between Roman society and the contractual system.

At this stage I should like to emphasise that we have been concerned only with very basic points of the contractual system. We have not looked critically at lesser matters, however important they might be. There has been no need. But the absence of any such discussion is the result of deliberate choice and is not due to a lack of material. Three examples will make this plain.

First, the agreement of the parties is central to a contract, and especially to a consensual contract which is created without formalities. But there is a scarcity of information on some aspects of agreement. Thus, it is by no means clear what degree of error was sufficiently grave to prevent the creation of a contract of sale.[33] Nor does any text discuss the effect of drunkenness on the formation of intention in any contract (or even in marriage).[34] Yet error and drunkenness, separately or even together, must surely have been common. Again, it is not clear whether for a contract of mandate to come into existence the parties must intend to enter a legal relationship.[35]

Secondly, Roman private law never recognised the outstandingly useful principle of direct representation, not even in the time of Justinian. Yet it must have been well-known to the jurists, especially from the example of Egypt which was under Roman rule from the time of Augustus. Thus, if we consider only sales, we find Romans in Egypt accepting direct agency from the second century A.D.[36]

Thirdly, the Roman contract of partnership, *societas*, was almost exclusively concerned with the relations of the partners *inter se*. When, on partnership business, one partner made a contract with a third party, the third party acquired rights against that partner alone. This always remained the case. Yet in bankers' partnerships, *societates argentariorum*, from at least the early first century B.C. a contract of one partner with a third party bound all of the partners.[37]

In respect of many areas of private law it might be argued that, though particular rules seem to us to be inefficient and out of step with society, nonetheless if we could only look at the rules from the standpoint of that society we would realise that they corresponded to the spirit of the people or the interests of the ruling élite. It was this argument which persuaded me that the first chapter on substantive law should be about contracts. People everywhere want the same basic things from their contract law: simplicity, efficiency and easiness of proof. There is no evidence that the Romans looked for anything else in their contract law or took any pride in what appear to us at least to be defects. That, as we have seen, the Romans were aware of the difficulties and tried in practice to obviate them where this was possible,[38] is enough to show that the Roman contractual system was out of step with Roman society.

Notes

1. On the *stipulatio* in general see, for all, Kaser, *RPR* 1, pp. 168ff, 538ff.
2. For an analysis of the functions of legal formalities see L. L. Fuller, 'Consideration and Form', *Columbia Law Review* 41 (1941), pp. 799ff.
3. For our purposes it is enough to refer to Kaser *RPR* 2, pp. 273ff, and the authorities he cites. The debate continues.
4. See, e.g. Kaser, *RPR* 1, pp. 168f and the authors he cites; Jolowicz-Nicholas, *Introduction*, pp. 280f.
5. See, e.g. G. Wissowa, *Religion und Kultus der Römer* 2nd edit. (Munich, Beck, 1912), p. 388. The censors (and before them presumably the kings) might mark with infamy an offender against the sacred.
6. See, e.g. Kaser, *RPR* 1, pp. 169f, and the authors he cites; Jolowicz-Nicholas, *loc. cit.* Some scholars see the *stipulatio* as having both these sacral and private law roots.
7. The fundamental works are by V. Arangio-Ruiz, now reprinted in his *Studi epigrafici e papirologici* edit. by L. Bove (Naples, Giannini, 1974), pp. 295ff, 309ff, 355ff, 518ff, 673ff; see also Watson, *Obligations*, pp. 22ff; Jolowicz-Nicholas, *Introduction*, pp. 282ff.
8. Cicero, *de off.* 3.14.58.
9. For a suggested origin of the contract which would explain the existence of the formal defect see Watson, *Obligations* pp. 22ff (apparently misunderstood by Jolowicz-Nicholas, p. 283 and n. 6).
10. See, e.g. Watson, *Obligations*, pp. 40f.
11. D.18.1.1.1 (*33 ad ed.*). There have been suggestions of interpolation in the text but see e.g. V. Arangio-Ruiz, *La compravendita in diritto romano* 2nd edit. (Naples, Jovene, 1956), pp. 90f. The question does not affect the present argument.
12. D.19.1.11.8 (Ulpian *32 ad ed.*); see F. de Zulueta, *The Roman Law of Sale* (Oxford, Clarendon Press, 1945), p. 44; Arangio-Ruiz, *Compravendita*, pp. 346f.
13. On the early history of this Edict see Watson, *Law Making*, pp. 82ff. The aediles were lesser magistrates who had to care, among other things, for the streets and market place. To do this they, like other Roman magistrates, issued regulations called edicts, and their regulations published as a writ are known as their Edict.
14. See, e.g. de Zulueta, *Sale*, pp. 46ff; Arangio-Ruiz, *Compravendita*, pp. 394ff.
15. It may be worth observing that Plato discusses implied warranties for sale in his *Laws* 11.915E, 916A, B, C.
16. See infra, p. 31ff.
17. A. Watson, 'The Origins of Consensual Sale: a Hypothesis', *T.v.R.* 32 (1964), pp. 245ff.

18. *Rhet. ad Herenn.* 2.13.19.
19. See, e.g. Watson, *Law Making*, pp. 31ff, 38.
20. See, e.g. Watson, *Obligations*, pp. 158ff; Kaser, *RPR* 1, p. 535.
21. *Coll.* 10.7.11.
22. For views which have been held on the nature of this action see Watson, *Obligations*, pp. 157f.
23. J. Burillo suggested that the edict was issued in two stages: 'Las fórmulas de la *actio depositi*', *SDHI* 28 (1962), pp. 233ff at pp. 245ff; contra, Watson, *Obligations*, pp. 160ff.
24. The obligation in mandate need not be to enter into a contract with a third person.
25. That there could be discussion as to the dividing line between *mandatum* and *depositum* appears from D.16.3.1.11–14.
26. For changes in vulgar law and Justinian's restoration of *mutuum* as a real contract see Kaser, *RPR* 2, pp. 270f.
27. But see e.g. M. Kaser, '*Mutuum* und *Stipulatio*', *Eranion Maridakis* 1 (Athens, Klissiounis, 1963), pp. 155ff.
28. G.4.53. From J.4.6.33 it would seem that relief was granted where the plaintiff was a minor, but otherwise only when the mistake was especially excusable.
29. D.18.1.1pr (Paul *33 ad ed.*).
30. G.3.141; D.18.1.1.1; 19.1.1pr (Paul *32* [*33*?] *ad ed.*); J.3.23.2.
31. On the use of Homer by both sides see above all D. Daube, 'Three Quotations from Homer in Digest 18.1.1.1', *CLJ* 10 (1949), pp. 213ff.
32. See, e.g. R. Monier, *Manuel de Droit romain, Les Obligations* 5th edit. (Paris, Domat Montchrestien, 1954), pp. 184ff; Buckland, *Textbook*, pp. 521ff; Kaser, *RPR* 1, pp. 580f.
33. See most recently R. Feenstra, 'The Dutch *Kantharos* Case and the History of *Error in Substantia*', *Tulane Law Review* 48 (1974), pp. 846ff.
34. See above all A. Watson, 'Drunkenness in Roman Law', *Sein und Werden im Recht (Festgabe von Lübtow)* edit. by W. G. Becker & L. S. von Carolsfield (Berlin, Duncker & Humblot, 1970), pp. 381ff.
35. See Watson, *Obligations*, pp. 148ff.
36. *P. Rainer* 25.817 (A.D. 189); *C.P.R.* 1.8 (A.D. 218); 1634 (A.D. 222); see R. Taubenschlag, *The Law of Graeco-Roman Egypt in the Light of the Papyri* 2nd edit. (Warsaw, Państwowe Wydawnictwo Naukowe, 1955), p. 311; cf. Watson, *Transplants*, p. 33.
37. *Rhet. ad Herenn.* 2.13.19; cf. D.2.14.25pr (Paul *3 ad ed.*); 2.14.27pr. (idem).
38. The legal scaffolding which develops to obviate difficulties is the subject of chapter 8: infra pp. 87ff.

Chapter 3

ROMAN LAW:
PATRIA POTESTAS

Patria potestas, the power of a Roman head of family over his children and remoter descendants, was the core of the Roman law of persons. In the second century A.D. the jurist Gaius could write:

Also in our *potestas* are the children whom we beget in civil marriage. This right is peculiar to Roman citizens; for scarcely any other men have over their sons a power such as we have. The late emperor Hadrian declared as much in the edict he issued concerning those who petitioned him for citizenship for themselves and their children. I am not forgetting that the Galatians regard children as being in the *potestas* of their parents.[1]

The unusual features of Roman *patria potestas* were both that it was so extensive and also that it ended only with the death of the *paterfamilias*. According to tradition the system was well organised as early as the days of Romulus who regulated it by legislation. *Patria potestas* was highly praised by the Greek writer, Dionysius of Halicarnassus, who lived in Rome from 30 B.C. and whose *Roman Antiquities* began to appear in 7 B.C.:

These then are the excellent laws which Romulus enacted concerning women, by which he rendered them more observant of propriety in relation to their husbands. But those he established with respect to reverence and dutifulness of children toward their parents, to the end that they should honour and obey them in all things, both in their words and actions, were still more august and of greater dignity and vastly superior to our (i.e. Greek) laws. ... Mild punishments are not sufficient to restrain the folly of youth and its stubborn ways or to give self-control to those who have been heedless of all that is honourable; and accordingly among the Greeks many unseemly deeds are committed by children against their parents. But the lawgiver of the Romans gave virtually full power to the father over the son, even during his whole life, whether he thought proper to imprison him, to scourge him, to put him in chains and keep him at work in the fields, or to put him to death, and this even though the son were already engaged in public affairs, though he were numbered among the highest magistrates, and though he were celebrated for his zeal for the commonwealth.[2]

We shall have to look more closely in a little while at the elements of *patria potestas*, but at this stage it is important to mention one aspect which, surprisingly, does not emerge from the quotation from Dionysius; a person in *potestas* could not own any property. It is immediately apparent to us that a system in which the majority of adults, even of the upper classes, males as well as females, could own no property but were dependent on their father or father's father, and were always subject to parental discipline, can scarcely have been economically satisfactory for the society as a whole. The main questions for us, therefore, are whether it corresponded to something deep in the Roman psyche, to the 'spirit of the people', and whether it worked to the advantage of the political élite.

The first thing to notice is that two devices developed early, *emancipatio* and the *peculium*, which profoundly modified the working of *patria potestas* though they had little effect on legal rules.

Emancipatio did not exist as early as the XII Tables, but was a new institution created apparently by the early guardians of the law, the pontiffs, by a deliberate misinterpretation of the provision of the XII Tables[3] that if a father sold his son three times the son was free from his father.[4] According to Gaius writing in the second century A.D., the father mancipates the son to a third party who in turn manumits the son *vindicta*. The son reverts to the father's *potestas*, and he mancipates the son again, and again the recipient manumits him. The process is repeated once again, and the son is then free from paternal power and independent. The XII Tables had spoken only of a son, and a very forced interpretation decided that only one mancipation would end *potestas* for all other descendants, male and female.[5] The procedure was clumsy – in the case of a son which would be the most common situation – but effective.

Thus *patria potestas* could be brought artificially to an end when the father wished. The need for such a possibility was obviously felt at a very early date and among the upper classes (who alone would have the necessary incentive,[6] and the necessary influence with the pontiffs) – but no statistical evidence is available to show how common the practice was. Some statistical evidence for the early post-classical period – when *patria potestas* was still in full swing – is, however, provided by Justinian's *Code*. For the period A.D. 235–284 for instance, there are 53 rescripts which deal in any way with parent and child and 14 of these show there was an *emancipatio*. For the succeeding reign of Diocletian the corresponding figures are 112 and 36. Since there may in some of the cases have been an *emancipatio* which is not mentioned because irrelevant, and since some of the rescripts concern infants, adoption and other topics, it emerges that at that time *emancipatio* was very common indeed.[7] The precise significance of this is not easy to judge. It may be that as a consequence of the *constitutio Antoniniana* which extended Roman citizenship to most of the free inhabitants of the Empire, a large proportion of the population – unused to Roman tradition – preferred to opt out of the system of *patria potestas*, and that *emancipatio* became much commoner. At the very least, however, one can say that during the third century A.D. very many Romans preferred not to live with the much vaunted *patria potestas*.

The other device modifying *patria potestas* is very much more important. Only persons, male or female, not subject to another's power could own property. But from very early times, fathers allowed their sons a fund (called a *peculium*) which they dealt with virtually as if it were their own. *Peculia* for free descendants are not evidenced in the XII Tables, but *peculia* to slaves are;[8] hence *a fortiori, peculia* to descendants existed. All the evidence suggests that in historical times, virtually every (male?) person in *patria potestas* – apart from the large class of have-nots[9] – had a *peculium*. Though the *peculium* existed and had legal recognition, there was little legal content to the *peculium*. Its legal recognition is apparent, above all, in the *actio de peculio et de in rem verso* and in *praelegata* of *peculium*. The *actio de peculio* which was probably invented in the first century B.C.[10] was a modified action brought against a *paterfamilias* in respect of a contract made by someone in his *potestas* or ownership. The *pater* could be condemned to pay damages up to the amount in the *peculium* and to the extent to which he had benefited.[11] Until the introduction of this action and the other *actiones adiecticiae qualitatis* (as such modified actions are called) no contractual remedy lay against a *paterfamilias* for contracts entered into by his dependants. This must have restricted the commercial usefulness of sons and slaves very severely. A *praelegatum* was a legacy left to an heir when there were more heirs than one. Commonly each heir who was in the *potestas* of the testator was left a *praelegatum* of his *peculium*.

The inability of a person in *potestas* to own property of his own should be the aspect of *patria potestas* of greatest social importance. Yet so far were the wealthier Roman citizens from accepting the values inherent in their much vaunted life-long power of the father that they evaded the effects by granting *peculia*. The resulting situation, however, can scarcely be regarded as satisfactory. If a son, of whatever age, made a contract with a third party and failed to perform adequately, that third party could not enforce against him a judgement for financial compensation since the son owned no property.[12] Again even when a son was granted the right of full administration of his *peculium* this did not entitle him to make gifts.[13] And when he died, no property rights passed since he owned no property. In keeping with this, a son, a *filiusfamilias*, could not make a will. Augustus made the first breach in this – a minor one, as Daube emphasises[14] – by ordaining that a *filiusfamilias* who was in the army could dispose of his soldier's pay and booty by will; but he lost this right when he left the service.[15] So far as property is concerned, it is no exaggeration to claim that in practice the Roman citizens largely abandoned the pure conception of *patria potestas* without putting in its place a system which was really satisfactory, economically or socially.

In evaluating *patria potestas* as a reflection of the spirit of the Roman people, some aspects should be stressed more than others. It is, of course, true – at least for periods in Roman history – that new-born infants might legally be exposed and left to die, that infants and young children might be sold into slavery by indigent parents, that parental consent might be required for marriage and might control divorce, and that fathers might have the legal right to punish recalcitrant children, and that all these are very important aspects of *patria potestas*. But all these are commonly to be found in other systems and would not justify Gaius' opinion of *patria potestas* as unique, or our singling out *patria potestas* as something peculiarly Roman. What does require our attention, apart from questions of property, are those elements which are very uncommon in other systems (or not found at all) and which give the *pater* extreme powers especially over adult descendants. Three elements appear particularly striking: the power of life and death, the power of sale into real slavery, and the right to surrender a wrongdoing descendant to the victim instead of paying compensation or a penalty.

The frequency of use and the extent of the power of life and death have been exaggerated in ancient times by the Greek Dionysius of Halicarnassus and in modern times by various scholars. Dionysius[16] and more recently E. Sachers[17] both list among instances of its use cases where a Roman commander put to death his own son for military insubordination which was a capital crime.[18] Again Dionysius[19] and many modern scholars write as if the father's power of life and death was unrestricted; but in fact there is textual evidence that the XII Tables themselves contained a clause that the *pater-familias* could put a son to death only with good reason,[20] which presumably would mean that the son had to have committed a serious crime.[21]

The father's power to sell 'across the Tiber' certainly existed but we seem to have no record of the power ever having been used. Cicero talks as if the power existed in his day,[22] but this may have been so only in theory. It is hard to resist the conclusion that in practice the right became obsolete long before the Empire.[23]

The right to surrender a son, daughter, or remoter descendant instead of paying compensation or the penalty for a delict committed by the descendant also existed but the right to surrender a female had disappeared by the time of Gaius,[24] and the surrender of males was abolished by Justinian.[25] We cannot tell how often the right was used. Though it does seem to have existed in practice in classical law,[26] Justinian tells us that it was obsolete before he abolished it. Noxal surrender of free persons must always have been very rare.

The threat of using the extremer powers of *patria potestas* can scarcely have been very real. At this point it seems appropriate to return to the subject of the *peculium*. The *peculium* belonged to the *pater* who had the right to take it back arbitrarily from his descendant at any time. Nowhere in any text, legal or lay, do we actually find this happening. Indeed, an argument from silence can take us very much further. If *patria potestas* had had the social importance which is given it in modern accounts, then the most important social fact about anyone, especially any adult male, would be whether he was or was not in *patria potestas*. Yet as one reads the surviving non-legal Roman writings one is hardly ever made aware of a person's status in this regard. However, we learn incidentally and with surprise that the infamous praetor and governor of Sicily, C. Verres, was a *filiusfamilias*,[27] a fact which did not prevent him amassing fortunes. In general, though, the Roman lay authors write as if *patria potestas* was not a fact of life.

When we turn to Roman political life, we find that all elected posts were equally open to *filii* and *patresfamiliarum*. The importance of this is that we cannot say that the system of *patria potestas* was maintained in the economic interest of the ruling élite. Daube, how-ever, stresses that the expenses of campaigning for election were such that a *filius* could not finance himself from his *peculium* but would require the specific support of his *pater*.[28] There must be truth in that, but it is not the whole story. *Peculia* in some cases could have been very large. The main objection, though, to Daube's point is that it is not *patria potestas* which should be blamed for the *filius'* shortage of money. The same factual situation would apply in any society where gentlemen from well-to-do families do not usually earn their living by trade, commerce or industry. This was commonly the case until very recent years. Readers of Anthony Trollope will remember the effect of the Dean of Barchester's threat to cut off the allowance of his son, Major Grantly, V.C., who was by no means a callow boy below the age of majority. Yet *The Last Chronicle of Barset* is set in nineteenth century England where the Roman *patria potestas* did not exist. In any family which derives its income from property, children remain economically dependent so long as their father is alive, unless they acquire a trade. If this be considered unworthy of a gentleman, independence is in practice impossible for the children of the aristocracy, whatever their legal position may be.

Similarly, one does not have to postulate *patria potestas* to envisage a man, in the grip of moneylenders, killing his father in order to inherit. But the effect of an episode of that sort in the midfirst century A.D. was the *senatusconsultum Macedonianum* which laid down that a person who lent money to a *filiusfamilias* could not sue for repayment, not even when the *filius* became independent of paternal power. The commercial inconvenience of such a rule is easily imagined.

All in all, it seems to me that *patria potestas* was harmful to the Roman economy and not at all beneficial to the ruling élite. The system was fundamentally inconvenient and remained so despite everything which could be done to mitigate its effects. Yet *patria potestas* does not seem to have corresponded to any deep-felt need in the Roman psyche. It could be, and frequently was, artificially terminated by *emancipatio*, and its most far-reaching social consequence, that *filii* could have no property, was very largely negatived by the virtually universal grant of a *peculium*. The extreme powers of the *pater* are scarcely in evidence. The adherence of the Romans in the later Republic and the Empire to the concept of *patria potestas* can scarcely be described as reasonable.

Before leaving this chapter we should consider the view of Daube.[29] He also emphasises the inconvenience of *patria potestas* but concludes:[30]

The principal explanation of the tenacity with which the Roman upper classes – for it is only a question of that minority – stuck to these incredible rules is that they saw them as expressing, and safeguarding, their innate superiority over the foreign rabble and probably, in course of time, also over the rabble at home. There is no limit to the hardship people will bear for the sake of status, national or sectional. Here lies the clue, and if only we look, the sources contain a good many corroborative hints. Gaius, for instance, repeatedly stresses that *patria potestas* is more exclusively Roman than other institutions which, under Roman law, apply to citizens only: it is found, he declares, among practically no other men. Hadrian himself attached great weight to the exclusiveness of the institution. In this feeling a *filiusfamilias*, however inconvenient his condition, was united with his Head. The rarity of emancipation, adverted to above, certainly has something to do with this. The better citizens were proud of this grotesque family structure.

This is ingenious but not, I find, wholly persuasive. The surprising fact – if *patria potestas* had the cachet Daube attaches to it – is that its uniqueness is actually very little stressed in the legal sources. And there is no evidence that *emancipatio* was rare in classical law – in the third century when evidence is available *emancipatio* is fre-. quent. There is also no evidence, I think, that the better citizens were proud of their grotesque family structure. The survival of *patria potestas*, inconvenient though that institution was, is simply to be seen as another instance where law came to be wildly out of step both with the needs of the society and the life-style of the society, its leaders included. It is a supreme example of the power of inertia.

Notes

1. G.1.55.
2. 2.26.
3. See, e.g. D. Daube, 'Texts and Interpretation in Roman and Jewish Law', *Jewish Journal of Sociology* 3 (1961), pp. 3ff at p. 5; Jolowicz-Nicholas, *Introduction*, pp. 89f; Kaser, *RPR* 1, pp. 68f.
4. For the original purpose of this clause see now Watson, *Rome of the XII Tables*, pp. 117ff.
5. G.1.132.
6. See infra, p. 28.
7. See A. Watson, 'Private Law in the Rescripts of Carus, Carinus and Numerianus', *T.v.R.* 41 (1973), pp. 19ff at pp. 23f.
8. See now Watson, *Rome of the XII Tables*, pp. 91ff.
9. See infra, p. 28.
10. See Watson, *Obligations*, pp. 185ff.
11. See in general, Buckland, *Textbook*, pp. 533ff.
12. We need not go into the details of the availability of contractual actions against *filii*, but no such action lay against a woman who

was *alieni iuris*, a slave or a person *in mancipio*: G.3.104; see Kaser, *RPR* 1, p. 343.

13. See, e.g. D. Daube, *Roman Law, Linguistic, Social and Philosophical Aspects* (Edinburgh, 1969), pp. 83f.
14. *Roman Law*, p. 78.
15. J.2.12pr; for subsequent developments see Buckland, *Textbook*, pp. 280f.
16. 2.26.6; 8.79.2.
17. *Realencyclopaedie der classischen Altertumswissenschaft* 22, 1046ff.
18. See already R. Yaron, '*Vitae necisque potestas*', *T.v.R.* 30 (1962), pp. 243ff at pp. 243f.
19. 2.26.4ff.
20. *Gai Inst. fr. Augustod.* 85, 86.
21. For the argument and modern literature see Watson, *Rome of the XII Tables*, pp. 42f.
22. *de orat.* 1.40.181f; *pro Caecina* 34.98.
23. Cf. Buckland, *Textbook*, p. 103.
24. G.4.75ff.
25. J.4.8.6.
26. *Coll.* 2.3.
27. Cicero, *in Verrem* II.1.23.60f; cf. Watson, *Obligations*, p. 37; Daube, *Roman Law*, p. 85.
28. *Roman Law*, pp. 84f.
29. *Roman Law*, pp. 75ff.
30. Pp. 85f.

Chapter 4

ROMAN LAW:
FURTHER POINTS

In the preceding two chapters we looked at fundamental weaknesses in the Roman system of contracts and the inconveniences of *patria potestas*. A similar look at other branches of law would show, I believe, equally grave defects where law was and remained for a very long time badly out of step with society. But instead of choosing one further field of law for appraisal I should like to consider first in this chapter some important legal distinctions, then some additional points. Both the practice and the growth of law are largely a matter of drawing distinctions, and the quality of a legal system is to a considerable extent a function of the quality of the distinctions which are made. We shall look at the major distinction in the law of private property, namely that between *res mancipi* and *res nec mancipi*; the most important one in theft (which is also one of the most striking in the law of delict), that between *furtum manifestum* and *furtum nec manifestum*; and one in marriage of little practical interest but of great significance, that between marriage with a brother's daughter and marriage with a sister's daughter.

Property which could be privately owned was either a *res mancipi* or a *res nec mancipi*. *Res mancipi* were land and houses on Italic land, slaves, animals commonly broken to draught or burden namely oxen, horses, mules and asses, and rustic praedial servitudes.[1] All other things were *res nec mancipi*. Ownership of *res mancipi* could be transferred only by the ceremony of *mancipatio* or by the modification of an action, *cessio in iure*, in front of a magistrate.[2] Ownership of corporeal *res nec mancipi* could be transferred by simple delivery, *traditio*.

The ceremony of *mancipatio* required the presence of five witnesses and a person who held the bronze scales, all of whom had to be Roman citizens of full age. The transferee grasped with one hand the object to be mancipated, for instance a slave, and he held a piece of bronze in the other. He declared, necessarily in Latin, 'Hunc ego hominem ex iure Quiritium meum esse aio isque mihi emptus esto hoc aere aeneaque libra', 'I declare that this slave is mine in accordance with the law of the citizens, and let him have been bought by me with this bronze and these bronze scales'. He struck the scales with the bronze and handed it to the seller as a symbolic price. Land, but only land, could be mancipated at a distance.

The origins of *mancipatio* are very obscure. Several theories have been brought forward to explain why the witnesses are five or, alternatively, why so many as five are needed, why the transferor says nothing, why the transferee has to lay hold of the thing, and why his declaration begins with an assertion of ownership, and only later proceeds with 'let him have been bought by me'. And 'emptus esto' at that time could probably mean 'let him have been taken', just as easily as 'let him have been bought'.[3] In the circumstances we should not attempt to settle these questions in this book, but we should assume that the arrangements for *mancipatio* were sensible at the time of its creation.[4] [In this we are following the course which was tacitly adopted in chapter two. When dealing with an institution or rule which extends back into dim antiquity and whose origins are not clear, we must proceed on the basis that the institution or rule came into being in a wholly rational way. As we shall see when we come to deal with an institution or rule whose history is apparent from the beginning, this is not always true. But as a matter of method we have no choice especially in a work whose aim is to show that law is to a considerable extent out of step with society.] In any event, whether the business with the scales was an original part of *mancipatio* or (as some think) a later addition, it must refer to an actual weighing of copper or bronze, and date to a time before the introduction of coined money.

Not only should we assume that *mancipatio* was originally a sensible arrangement, but we should also praise the skill of the lawyers who adapted it to many functions: for making a will, for marriage (*coemptio*), for creating real security (*fiducia*), for adoption, for emancipating a descendant from paternal power.[5] But it cannot be claimed that, as a conveyance, *mancipatio* was at all rational after the very early days right up until the distinction between *res mancipi* and *res nec mancipi* was abolished by Justinian.[6]

The business with copper and scales may be left aside as a harmless anachronism. Clearly, weighing the metal was no longer functional after the introduction of coinage, but this part of the ceremony need not distress us.[7] The same cannot be said for the requirement that the appropriate words had to be spoken in Latin.[8] In many parts of the Empire, including some of the richest like Egypt, Latin would be known by only a small proportion of the inhabitants. Needless difficulties would then exist for honest citizens. Again, whatever the original reason for requiring five citizen witnesses and another to hold the scales, the number is unnecessarily large for the simple task of witnessing and providing evidence of the transaction. In certain country districts it might be difficult to find enough qualified witnesses who could easily be brought together. Moreover, if even one witness was mistakenly thought to be a citizen the *mancipatio* would be void. It seems that where marriage was concerned mistakes in status were common.[9] One would expect that couples who married would know each other's background; *a fortiori* mistakes in the status of witnesses for *mancipatio* would not be uncommon.

Then the dividing line between those things which were *res mancipi* and those which were not ceased to have – if it ever had – any rational purpose. Valuable things of many types never came to be classed as *res mancipi*; elephants, camels, gold, silver, precious stones, land and houses outside Italy. Indeed, it is clear that the Romans did not always understand where the dividing line was drawn. Thus in Pliny the Elder we come across the *mancipatio* of emeralds and pearls,[10] from Transylvania where the land was not Italic we have a document recording the sale and *mancipatio* of half of a house in A.D. 159.[11]

Mancipatio as a conveyance would lose much of its value with the introduction of the *actio Publiciana*, whether this is to be dated in the first century B.C. or not until the first century A.D.[12] This action gave a person who received a *res mancipi* without *mancipatio* and who lost possession of it the right to recover it if he would have become owner had the period of usucapion run.[13] Henceforward in practical terms his position was little different from that of a true owner, except that until he actually became owner he could not free a slave. Thenceforward the continuing distinction between *res mancipi* and *res nec mancipi* has an air of unreality, and the law seems unnecessarily complex. But one aspect of the distinction did remain important. *Mancipatio* by itself gave the buyer a guarantee against eviction for double the price stated in the *mancipatio*; no guarantee against eviction was inherent in transfer of ownership by simple delivery.

To whose advantage did *mancipatio* operate? Not, after the very early days at least, for the protection of the family of the transferor. Nor for any particular class of society; it was socially neutral.[14] With its built-in warranty it did favour the buyer rather than the seller,[15] but there is no social class of buyers and another of sellers of *res mancipi*. Since it was part of the *ius civile* it could be used only by those who had *commercium* and hence was not available to transfer civil law ownership to a peregrine. But this, too, would scarcely have much practical, rational point, or even be disadvantageous to peregrines after Roman court protection of peregrines' rights was afforded sometime early in the Republic.[16] Moreover, if *mancipatio* did favour one powerful group rather than another weaker one, why did the law not come to recognise more things as *res mancipi*? All in all it is difficult to see social or class reasons for the retention of *mancipatio* and of *res mancipi* and *res nec mancipi*.

We have here an instance where law failed to change when the needs of society changed. Let us return to the frequently stated idea that there is a time-lag between change in society and the corresponding change in the law.[17] Such a time-lag in many circumstances is only to be expected and indeed is inevitable. But from at least the third century B.C. until its abolition in the sixth century A.D. the distinction between *res mancipi* and *res nec mancipi* no longer served a rational need or desire of society. When such a long time span is involved, it is meaningless to talk of a time-lag. It is not just that the law responded sluggishly to social change. For the greater part of the lifetime of Roman law there was no rational connection between Roman society and the main distinction in the law of property. Yet the centuries of stagnation here included the last two centuries of the Republic – the most fertile period of legal development in the world's history, I believe – and the famous centuries of classical law.

Before we leave *res mancipi* and *res nec mancipi* it should be observed that this example of separation of law and society is very different from most of those discussed in the chapter on contract. The inefficient formalities of *stipulatio* and the literal contract, the absence of inherent warranties against eviction and latent defects in sale and the lack of a contract of barter are all example of failure of law to develop sufficiently from the start to meet the social needs. The social needs and desires did not change; the law just did not develop – or not for centuries – to meet them, obvious though they were.

Fundamental to the law of theft is the distinction between manifest theft and non-manifest theft, *furtum manifestum* and *furtum nec manifestum*. Every theft was one or the other. The importance of the distinction lay in the penalty. For manifest theft the XII Tables laid down capital penalties.[18] A free man was scourged, and *addictio*, surrender, was made of him by the magistrate to the victim. A slave was scourged and thrown from the Tarpeian rock. The Praetor substituted a penalty of four times the value of the stolen property in both these cases, in the Republic for free men, but not until the Empire for slaves.[19] For non-manifest theft the action from the earliest times was for double the value of the stolen property,[20] whether the wrongdoer was a free man or a slave.[21]

Yet what was this distinction and what was its reason or purpose? What the distinction was is by no means certain. The etymology of *manifestum* is obscure. Presumably the first element is from *manus*, 'hand' – though even that has been doubted[22] – presumably in the ablative, but the *festus* element is a complete mystery. Nor do we know whether the adjective was attached originally to the thief or the theft. Was it the thief who was manifest, or was the theft manifest? The XII Tables admittedly attach the adjective to the theft.[23] But from Plautus we learn that – at least by his time and why not earlier? – it could be the thief who was manifest,[24] or even in comic terms another wrongdoer.[25] Moreoever, Plautus uses the adjective *manifestus* or the adverb *manufesto* also of acts other than theft where the idea of 'by the hand' or 'in the hand' or 'with the hand' had long gone. Thus, for instance, it is employed of a bare-faced lie and of a passionate kiss.[26] What we can be sure of is that the XII Tables did not explain the difference between manifest and non-manifest, or the problem facing the classical jurists would not have existed.

Thus in the second century A.D. the jurist Gaius wrote in his Institutes:

> 3.184 Manifest theft, according to some, is theft detected whilst being committed. Others extend it to theft detected in the place where it is committed, holding, for example, that a theft of olives commited in an olive-grove, or of grapes committed in a vineyard, is manifest if detected whilst the thief is still in the olive-grove or vineyard, or, where there is theft in a house, whilst the thief is still in the house. Others, going further, have maintained that a theft remains manifest up to when the thief has carried the thing to the place he intended. And others go so far as to say that it is manifest if the thief is seen at any time with the thing in his hands. This last opinion has not been accepted, nor does the opinion that the theft is manifest if detected before the thief has carried the thing to where he intended, seem to be approved, because it raises a considerable doubt as to whether this is to be limited to one day or extends to several, the point being that thieves often intend to carry off what they have stolen to another town or province. Either of the first two opinions is tenable, but the second is generally preferred.

And the Digest is as revealing for the distinction in classical law as in the age of Justinian.

47.2.3 (Ulpian *41 ad Sab.*) A *fur manifestus* is a thief who is what the Greek call ἐπ' αὐτοφώρῳ, that is one who is taken with the goods stolen. 1. Who takes him is a matter of small account; it may be the owner or it may be someone else. 2. It may however be asked whether he is only *manifestus* if he is taken in the act of stealing, or it is enough that he should be simply taken somewhere or other. On the whole – and this is held by Julianus – even though he should not be taken in the place where he committed the theft, still he is a *fur manifestus* if he is taken with the thing stolen in his possession before he has brought it to the place he intended.

47.2.4 (Paul *9 ad Sab.*) By 'the place a man intends to bring a thing to' is to be understood 'the place at which he intends to stop that day with those stolen goods'.

47.2.5 (Ulpian *41 ad Sab.*) Consequently whether he is taken on public or private ground, so long as he has not yet brought the thing to the place intended, his legal position is that of a *fur manifestus*, if he is taken with the stolen goods: this you may read in Cassius. 1. But, if he has once brought the thing to the place he intended, then, even though he should be taken with the thing, still he is not a *fur manifestus*.

47.2.6 (Paul *9 ad Sab.*) For though *furtum* may be committed over and over again by repeated acts of handling, still it was thought good to determine the question whether the thief is *manifestus* or not by reference to the commencement, that is, the time of the original theft.

47.2.7 (Ulpian *41 ad Sab.*) If a man commits *furtum* while a slave, but is only taken after manumission, is he a *fur manifestus*? According to Pomponius (ex Sabino lib. xix) he cannot be sued for *furtum manifestum*, as the original circumstances of the theft, committed as it was by a slave, do not make it *manifestum*. 1. In the same passage this author remarks with strict legal propriety that a thief is only made *manifestus* by being taken; further, if, while I was engaged in stealing goods from your house, you hid yourself for fear that I should kill you, then, though you saw the theft committed, still it is not a case of *furtum manifestum*. 2. However, Celsus holds that besides the case of taking there may be the following: suppose you see the man carrying something off and run to apprehend him, whereupon he throws the goods down and makes his escape, in this case he is a *fur manifestus*; 3. and it makes very little difference, in his opinion, whether the capture of a thief is by the owner or a neighbour or a casual passer-by.

Thus, throughout the classical period and even into the time of Justinian there was considerable doubt as to the dividing line between *furtum manifestum* and *furtum nec manifestum*. And yet because of its effect upon the penalty inflicted, the distinction was basic. More surprising still there was no discussion – so far as our sources go – of the reason for the distinction. So far as we can tell no classical jurist and none of Justinian's compilers ever asked himself or anyone else, 'Why do we draw a distinction between *furtum manifestum* and *furtum nec manifestum*?'

Some modern scholars have considered the question and they have come up with two main theories. One is that there may be an element of doubt about the accused's guilt in *furtum nec manifestum* but there is none in *furtum manifestum*.[27] If this view is correct, as it may be, then there was a degree of illogicality in drawing the distinction. Doubt as to guilt may be a good reason for not condemning in the action, but not for fixing a lower penalty. The other theory takes various forms but is based on the idea that in an early society a victim who catches a thief in the act is likely to kill him. The original rules on *furtum manifestum* were, therefore, society's attempt to institutionalise this self-help and bring it within the control of the state. The four-fold penalty introduced by the Praetor would then be a further step away from personal vengeance, and the high pecuniary damages would be justified since the wrongdoer's life was being spared.[28] If this view is correct then it is all the more astounding that the distinction never disappeared.[29]

This, then, is the distinction between *furtum manifestum* and *furtum nec manifestum*. Drawn as early as the fifth century B.C., it was of enormous practical importance for every theft since it determined the extent of the penalty, and it flourished even in the law of Justinian. Yet what exactly the distinction was was never wholly apparent. Its purpose and justification and the reason for drawing it are all lost in the mists of antiquity, and no Roman jurist in recorded history ever seems to have wondered about them.

The third example is of a very different nature and quality. But what it lacks in frequency of daily application it makes up for in psychological impact. It is often felt that family law above all corresponds to the spirit of the people, or has a 'legitimately native character'. For instance, for this reason it has been claimed that family law is extremely resistant to change due to foreign influence.[30] At the emotional heart of family law lie the prohibited degrees of relationship for marriage; thus it is usually claimed that incest is an offence recognised in all systems[31] and is the only offence of such universality. Against this background we must consider the marriage between the Emperor Claudius and his niece, Agrippina, in A.D. 49 and the consequences. Tacitus reports[32] that rumour and their illicit passion predicted that marriage was arranged between Claudius and Agrippina. But they did not dare to celebrate the rites of marriage since there was no example of a girl being married by her father's brother. 'Indeed that was incestuous, and it was feared that disregard might bring national disaster.' Vitellius arranged that the Senate demand that Claudius and Agrippina marry. Claudius accepted at once and 'entered the Senate to request a decree that, also in the future, marriage would be lawful between uncles and the daughters of brothers'.[33] More soberly, about a century later, the jurist Gaius states the law:[34]

> A man may lawfully marry his brother's daugher, a practice introduced after the late emperor Claudius married Agrippina his brother's daughter. But to marry one's sister's daughter is unlawful. These rules are declared by imperial constitutions.

Here then is the distinction that concerns us. In the first century A.D., marriage with a brother's daughter became lawful, marriage with a sister's daughter remained unlawful. The innovation permitting marriage with a brother's daughter was not due to a changed view of kinship or blood-ties, but was solely a political move, gratifying the lust of one man. Tacitus and, to a lesser extent, Suetonius emphasise that until Claudius' passion for Agrippina, sexual relations between uncle and niece were regarded as horrible incest.

Yet once the decree of the senate was passed permitting marriage with a brother's daughter, that remained the law for almost three hundred years. Apart from any question of people's instinctive revulsion against incest three factors make this topic of compelling interest. First, the distinction between permitted marriage with brother's daughter and forbidden marriage with sister's daughter is irrational and does not correspond to anything inherent in the Roman attitude to blood relationships, yet the distinction remained for a very long time unaltered and, indeed, so far as we can tell, unquestioned. This is all the more striking in that the famous classical period of Roman law had begun and was to continue for two more centuries. Were the jurists incapable of noticing or of responding to the illogicality? Secondly, the strange innovation was made to satisfy Claudius. But the unanimous verdict of subsequent Romans was that Claudius was very eccentric, and dominated by his wives and freedmen: he was not renowned for balanced judgement. One might have thought that his legal innovations –

particularly this one, illogical in itself, and moreover subjecting him to the dominance of Agrippina – would not be treated as sacrosanct, but judged on merit. This does not seem to have happened. Thirdly, there are the terms of the rescript of the Emperors Constantius and Constans which abolished the distinction on March 31, 342:[35]

> If anyone should be so abominable as to believe that the daughter of his brother or sister should be made his wife, or should fly to her embrace not as her paternal or maternal uncle, he will be liable to a penalty of capital punishment.

Thus, the distinction was abolished by making marriage with a brother's daughter once again illegal. So terrible did incest with a niece seem that the penalty introduced was death. It might be suggested that it was the new spirit of Christianity, not the old Roman spirit, which found marriage with a brother's daughter intolerable, but I doubt whether the suggestion would be convincing. To begin with, we know that the Romans had previously regarded such relations as incestuous and fearsome. Sooner or later – later rather than sooner – a change was bound to come either to make such marriages again void or to permit marriage with a sister's daughter. Then again there is no scriptural authority for the view that sexual relationships with a niece are incest. Indeed, sex between uncle and niece has never been regarded as incestuous in Jewish law.[36] Nor is there evidence from before 342 that such was the Christian view. Christianity, at the very most, could have been a subsidiary contributory factor.

Before leaving this subject, we should consider the possible objection to the foregoing discussion of marriage with a niece, that the law remained unchanged between 49 and 342 precisely because uncles and nieces do not marry and the rules were of no practical significance. To such an argument – which is certainly not without force – one would reply in the first instance that that does not affect the illogicality of the legal rules. There would be something all the more pathetic in jurists like Gaius expounding to their students that marriage with a brother's daughter was valid, with a sister's daughter void. Moreover, one should set against the presumed absence of practical significance the assumed emotional response to improper sex. Did the Romans continue to find even the theoretical idea of sex with a sister's daughter so abhorrent that such marriages were forbidden, but had no frisson of horror over marriage with a brother's daughter? Finally although marriage with a niece cannot have been common we know that it did occur. In discussing Claudius' marriage, Suetonius claims there were only two other instances, and Tacitus records one which may be the same as one in Suetonius. These writers would wish to make Claudius' marriage seem as exceptional as they possibly could.

Finally it should be observed that the innovation of A.D. 49 which introduced the irrational distinction is different from any other instance which we have so far considered of a divergence between law and society. Not only do we know why it was introduced, but we can see that *from the outset* the distinction was neither rational nor in tune with the outlook of society, but was due entirely to the efforts of a pressure group. The same senators, moreover, would have favoured any different rule of law if that would have enabled them to please Claudius. In slightly altered circumstances, one could easily imagine that the decree of the senate would have allowed marriage with a sister's daughter, but not with a brother's daughter.

It would be possible to give many more examples – fundamental ones at that – where Roman law was badly out of step with Roman society. But to be sufficiently systematic it is not necessary, I believe, to go through the whole of that legal system. A few further instances might, however, with profit be mentioned here. Thus on intestate succession, the provision of the XII Tables that if there was no *suus heres* (i.e. a person in the *potestas* or *manus* of the deceased who became *sui iuris* by his death), the nearest agnate, *agnatus proximus*, was to have the inheritance, was interpreted very narrowly. 'Agnatus proximus' was taken to mean the nearest agnate alive when the *de cuius* died. If this agnate died before he accepted the inheritance or if – as was possible in Roman law – he refused the inheritance, succession did not open to the next nearest agnate, but the right to inherit went straight to the *gentiles*, the members of the clan. This restricted interpretation was by no means dictated by the words 'agnatus proximus'. Probably the provision of the XII Tables was an innovation – previously *sui* and *gentiles* alone being entitled to succeed on intestacy – hence the narrow interpretation in favour of the *gentiles*.[37] But once the interpretation was made it remained, and the situation was only altered by the *edictum Unde cognati* which probably still did not exist in the seventies B.C.[38] Until the edict was issued succession by the *gentiles* remained common.[39] Yet by then, the *gentes* had for centuries ceased to have much real significance. Who can doubt that for hundreds of years the propertied Roman would have preferred close relatives to succeed rather than the distant – and, in fact, very shadowy – *gentiles*? Moreover, the rules of the XII Tables continued to exist long after the introduction of edicts so that the whole law of intestate succession was extremely confused and confusing.

From testate succession we may choose to look at legacies which might be left in one of several forms. One common form is that known as legacy *per vindicationem*. For this form to be valid, as we know from Gaius[40] writing in the second century A.D., the object legated had to be owned by the testator at the moment he made the will as well as when he died. The former requirement must go back to a time when the legacy was not created by a will which had effect only when the testator died. That is, it must have originated – and only makes sense – at the period when a Roman who wished to order the disposition of his property after death went through a *mancipatio* ceremony which did not count as a true will but which, seemingly or technically or fictitiously at least, transferred the property at once. But the XII Tables of about 451 B.C. had expressly confirmed (Tab. V.3) the validity of arrangements so made as regulating succession on death. Even if it would be an anachronism to think that this clause of the code made a true will out of the *mancipatio* ceremony the recognition of such a will could not be long delayed.[41] The requirements of *legata per vindicationem* caused inconveniences which were so strongly felt that often testators would leave the same thing to the same legatee in two different ways. This practice in turn presented the jurists with nice problems of interpretation, whether or not to treat the two legacies as cumulative.[42]

Again, from contract we may look at novation. This was the transformation of an obligation created by stipulation into a new stipulatory obligation. The parties made a new stipulation in which the same basic debt remained but something new was added. The old stipulation was extinguished. Now Gaius reports a very strange dispute about the effect of novation when a condition was to be added to a stipulation.[43] In his time novation took place only if the condition was realised; if it failed the previous obligation continued. This is clearly contrary to the intention of the parties. At the time they make the novatory stipulation the intention is undoubtedly that the obligation is to be enforceable only if the condition is fulfilled. If the simple stipulatory promise to pay 5,000 sesterces is transformed into a promise to pay 5,000 sesterces if Gorbulio wins the next chariot race, it can scarcely be argued that what the parties wanted and agreed on was that if Gorbulio arrived last, the second stipulation was to be discounted and the first was to be enforceable. The jurists were, of course, aware of this and Gaius says 'Let us see (videamus) whether one who sues on the obligation can not be defeated by the defence of fraud or the defence of pact'. However he does not discuss the question, and it is likely that he is using the verb 'videamus' to indicate that in his view the question is open.[44] Gaius then goes on to relate that Servius – a famous jurist of two centuries earlier – had held that novation took place at once, even during the pendency of the condition, and that if the condition failed no action lay on either stipulation so that all claim was lost. This obviously does correspond to the parties' intention. But what were the classical jurists' playing at? Their interpretation that novation took place only when the condition was fulfilled is not necessary, is contrary to the intention of the parties, and is highly artificial when allowance is made for the special defences of fraud and pact. Presumably their attitude was based on some theoretical considerations and was dictated by love of or pride in the technicalities of their craft. Possibly the argument was that the first obligation continued until there was a second obligation, and that there was no new obligation until the condition happened. The legal rules actually to operate could have been envisaged in one of two ways by the jurists responsible for the change. First the jurists might have considered that if the condition failed and the old obligation continued the party founding on it could always be rebutted by the defence of fraud or pact. That is, despite what was said above, it was not and never had been an open question whether these special defences were available.[45] If this were the case, then the justists' new attitude would have little real effect in practical terms on the law. Their attitude would primarily have made the law more technical, and more difficult for the non-specialist Roman to approach and understand. A further wedge would have been driven between the law and the people. Secondly, the jurists might have considered that if the new condition failed the old obligation continued and an action brought on it would succeed. If this were so, then their decision would negative the intention of the parties.

If the sole purpose of this book had been to show that in at least one major system there was a very considerable divergence between the rules of private law and what was efficacious for the society and what was desired by and desirable for the people or their leaders, we could probably stop here. None of the existing theories of legal development or of the relationship between law and society take into account or can take into account the enormous extent to which Roman law diverged from the needs of Roman society. Since these theories postulate a pattern of development or a relationship between law and society which is common to all systems – or for Maine (who is not in point here) to all early systems – and which is necessary, the existence of even one major system which to a very considerable extent falls outside of the theories presents an insuperable objection to them. Once again it should be emphasised that I am not denying and have no wish to deny that most, and perhaps all, of these theories contain more than a grain of truth. From Roman law itself we could with no difficulty find examples where the simplest explanation of a particular legal rule would be that it corresponded to the spirit of the people; clear cases of social engineering, and equally plain instances where the rule was conceived of, and actually was, in the interests of the economic élite. That reality does correspond to some extent, even perhaps to a great extent to one or more of these theories is, however, not proof of the validity of the theory. The fact that some swans are black would not constitute proof of a theory that all swans were of necessity black.

In the chapters on Roman law I have tended to stress contracts and family law. The former because it is relatively easier to know what people want from contract law and because it could be simply demonstrated that laymen and jurists alike were aware of the defects in the law. The latter because of the common belief – whose accuracy need not here be investigated – that family law is the part most closely interwoven into the needs and desires of the society. In both of these areas the divergences between Roman law and Roman society were marked. This is so even when one considers only one period such as the famous first century A.D. of classical law. It would be possible at this stage to list some of the factors responsible for the divergences but this task is more appropriately reserved for later in the book. One matter I should, however, like to emphasise – the longevity of legal rules. Even when, as in the examples studied, a rule of law is actively out of step with its society, it may continue to exist for centuries. In an earlier work I considered a different matter, the ease with which law could be transported from one system to another, and the jurisprudential significance of this.[46] The basic conclusion might have been summarised as: 'However historically conditioned their origins might be, rules of private law in their continuing lifetime have no inherent close relationship with a particular people, time or place.' For a very different angle the power of survival of unsatisfactory rules offers confirmation of that conclusion.

Someone may suggest that the divergence between law and society to the extent which I have claimed is purely a Roman phenomenon. After all, it might be said, Roman law could be so easily transported to other and later systems simply because it was universal, and was not closely linked with the particular society which gave it birth. A person of that persuasion might find reasons for that supposed state-of-affairs in the attitudes of the Roman jurists. Roscoe Pound, for instance, claimed:

> Law may be conceived as a philosophically discovered system of principles which express the nature of things, to which, therefore, man ought to conform his conduct. Such was the idea of the Roman jurisconsult, . . .'[47]

The well-known characteristic of Roman juristic texts that economic and social matters are excluded from the discussion[48] could, it might be said, be because the jurists were largely unconcerned with such things. It therefore seems appropriate to turn from Roman law to English law which in its development has owed so much to decisions by judges on practical questions, and which is famous for its non-theoretical and non-abstract approach.

Notes

1. G.2.14a.
2. Probably *in iure cessio* was seldom used for the transfer of ownership of corporeals: see Watson, *Property*, pp. 20f.
3. See now A. Watson, '*Emptio*, "taking" ', *Glotta* 53 (1975), pp. 294ff.
4. For theories see Kaser, *RPR* 1, pp. 41ff, especially at pp. 45f, and the authorities cited, especially in nn. 30ff.
5. See, e.g. Watson, *Roman Private Law*, p. 61.
6. C.7.31.1.5.
7. One might, though, consider it hard that the ceremony might be declared inefficacious because the scales were not struck with the copper.
8. There is no evidence that even Greek was ever allowed at any time for a *mancipatio*.
9. Argued from G.1.65–75.
10. *Nat. Hist.* 9.58.117.
11. Bruns, no. 113.
12. For disagreement on dating see Watson, *Property*, pp. 104ff; Kaser *RPR* 1, p. 438.
13. See, e.g. O. Lenel, *Das Edictum perpetuum* 3rd edit. (Leipzig, Tauchnitz, 1927), pp. 169ff; Buckland, *Textbook*, pp. 192ff. The action was also available to a *bona fide* possessor.
14. Unless we hold that the wealthier and better advised a man was, the more likely he was to be able to make use of the technicalities of *mancipatio*. In that sense, all law, whatever the intention of its maker is for the advantage of the relatively well-off.

15. Even this should not be stressed. The liability for *auctoritas* could be avoided by not stating the price in the *mancipatio* or making it appear very low, 'uno nummo'; see, e.g. Kaser, *RPR* 1, p. 46. In any event the buyer is likely to have taken a stipulation against eviction; cf. supra, pp. 14f. Interestingly the stipulation for double was usually given not only for *res mancipi* but also for other things of value.

16. We need not enter into a discussion here of the date of the fiction 'Si civis Romanus esset', and of the respective jurisdiction of the urban praetor and peregrine praetor.

17. I should not here be taken as suggesting that legal change is never earlier than the change in society's attitudes.

18. See, e.g. G.3.189.

19. See Watson, *Obligations*, pp. 231ff.

20. That is, when the action was brought by an owner who had an interest. We need not concern ourselves here with other cases.

21. See, e.g. G.3.190.

22. See A. Ernout & A. Meillet, *Dictionnaire étymologique de la langue latine* (Paris, Klincksieck, 1959), p. 385.

23. XII Tab. VIII.16a.

24. See, e.g. *As.* 569; *Poe.* 785.

25. For instance, adulterers, *Poe.* 862.

26. *Ba.* 695; *Ps.* 1260.

27. See, e.g. Buckland, *Textbook*, p. 582.

28. See, e.g. H. Maine, *Ancient Law*, pp. 222f (in Everyman's Library edition, London, Dent, 1917).

29. For the literature on the question see D. Pugsley, '*Furtum* in the XII Tables', *Irish Jurist* 4 (1969), pp. 139ff. Pugsley's own bizarre theory need not be discussed. Another, earlier, view is to be found in Montesquieu, *De l'Esprit des Lois*, book 29, ch. 13. It is often claimed – most recently by J. A. C. Thomas, *The Institutes of Justinian* (Cape Town, Juta, 1975), p. 264 – that the distinction survived only because it was of little practical importance. A criminal action, not the delictal *actio furti*, would be used, it is said, because an indigent thief could not pay the multiple penalty demanded by the civil law action. This is unconvincing since many a thief would be a slave, and the *actio furti* would lie against his owner. Even if the slave owner had little money, it would be to the advantage of the victim to sue by the *actio furti* since if the slave's owner was not prepared to pay the penalty awarded he had to surrender the slave to the victim.

30. For an interesting bibliography on the topic see W. Müller-Freienfels, 'The Unification of Family Law', *AJCL* 16 (1968–69), pp. 175ff at p. 175, n. 2.

31. See, e.g. M. Mead, *s.v. Incest* in *International Encyclopedia of the Social Sciences* 7 (Macmillan, 1968), pp. 115ff, with bibliography. In English secular law incest was not a criminal offence before the

Punishment of Incest Act, 1908. But it was punishable by proceedings in the ecclesiastical courts.

32. *Ann.* 12.5ff.
33. 12.7. Cf. for all this Suetonius, *Claudius*, 26.3.
34. G.1.62.
35. C.Th. 3.12.1.
36. *Leviticus*, 18 and 20; *Mishnah, Macc.* 3.1. See also the recent English case of *Cheni (née Rodrigues) v. Cheni* 1962 3 All ER 873.
37. See now Watson, *Rome of the XII Tables*, pp. 66ff and the references given, p. 69, n. 52.
38. See now A. Watson, *Succession in the Later Roman Republic* (Oxford, 1971), pp. 183f.
39. For the argument and textual evidence see Watson, *Succession*, pp. 180f.
40. G.2.196; *Epit. Ulp.* 24.7. The *senatusconsultum Neronianum* of A.D. 64 had already provided that, when the legacy was made in a form not suited to it, it should be construed as in the most favourable form (i.e. *per damnationem*) if that would make it valid: G.2.197; *Epit. Ulp.* 24.11a.
41. See now Watson, *Rome of the XII Tables*, pp. 52ff.
42. Mr. John Barton kindly tells me that the Digest texts on *legata geminata* had considerable influence on the development of the English law of 'satisfaction of legacies by legacies'.
43. G.3.179.
44. Cf. on Gaius' use of 'videbimus', B. Nicholas, '*Videbimus*', *Synteleia Arangio-Ruiz* (Naples, Jovene, 1964), pp. 150ff.
45. Kaser, for instance, holds that the defence of pact was automatically available; *RPR* 1, p. 648.
46. *Legal Transplants*.
47. Of course, he does not leave this unqualified, but the rest of his statement does not materially affect the point for us: *Introduction to the Philosophy of Law*, 2nd edit. (New Haven, Yale University Press, 1954), p. 26. From a different perspective F. H. Lawson calls Roman law 'the most purely legal of all laws': 'Roman Law as an Organising Instrument', *Boston University Law Review* 46 (1966), pp. 181ff at p. 204.
48. Thus F. Schulz says that classical Roman 'legal writings ignore the genetic connexion between law and extra-legal matters. The politico-economic conditions underlying the establishment of a legal rule are nowhere described or even mentioned. No economic considerations enter the law. The economic meaning of a legal institution, the normal economic functions it is destined to fulfil, the economic reasons for its introduction – all these are set aside on principle as non-juristic'; *Principles of Roman Law* (Oxford, Clarendon Press, 1936), p. 24.

Chapter 5

ENGLISH LAW: REAL PROPERTY; TENURE AND REGISTRATION

There is no better way to begin looking at the long continuous development of English law and the traditional attitudes of lawyers than by pondering the words of William Blackstone uttered at the opening of the Vinerian lectures on October 25, 1758.

The mischiefs that have arisen to the public from inconsiderate alterations in our laws, are too obvious to be called in question; and how far they have been owing to the defective education of our senators, is a point well worthy the public attention. The common law of England has fared like other venerable edifices of antiquity, which rash and unexperienced workmen have ventured to new-dress and refine, with all the rage of modern improvement. Hence frequently its symmetry has been destroyed, its proportions distorted, and its majestic simplicity exchanged for specious embellishments and fantastic novelties. For, to say the truth, almost all the perplexed questions, almost all the niceties, intricacies, and delays (which have sometimes disgraced the English, as well as other courts of justice) owe their original not to the common law itself, but to innovations that have been made in it by acts of parliament, 'overladen (as Sir Edward Coke expresses it) with provisoes and additions, and many times on a sudden penned or corrected by men of none or very little judgment in law'. This great and well-experienced judge declares, that in all his time he never knew two questions made upon rights merely depending upon the common law; and warmly laments the confusion introduced by ill-judging and unlearned legislators. 'But if', he subjoins, 'acts of parliament were after the old fashion penned, by such only as perfectly knew what the common law was before the making of any act of parliament concerning that matter, as also how far forth former statutes had provided remedy for former mischiefs, and defects discovered by experience; then should very few questions in law arise, and the learned should not so often and so much perplex their heads to make atonement and peace, by construction of law, between insensible and disagreeing words, sentences, and provisoes, as they now do'. And if this inconvenience was so heavily felt in the reign of Queen Elizabeth, you may judge how the evil is increased in later times, when the statute book is swelled to ten times a larger bulk: unless it should be found, that the penners of our modern statutes have proportionably better informed themselves in the knowledge of the common law.[1]

With his emphasis on the 'majestic simplicity' of the Common Law and the distorting effect of statute Blackstone appears almost as an early-day Savigny. The same scholar on the same occasion expressly tells us where to begin, with the gentlemen of independent estates and fortunes and with their landed property. Thus, our starting point can be land law. It should not be disputed that the legal rules were developed with the interests of the nobility and landed gentry in mind.[2] Indeed, the law of property, on the conventional view of the matter, should of all branches of law be the one which might be expected to reflect most accurately the interests of the possessing classes. It is of no concern to those who have no property, and those who do have property normally have influence as well. At the outset we must concede this for the land law as it existed in Blackstone's time, that it was an extremely flexible system, which in the hands of a master could produce almost any result which an aristocratic landowner could wish. But that is rather less than half of the story. It is true that the rich can afford to pay for the services of the best conveyancers, but even the rich can hardly be expected to take pleasure in doing so. Moreover, in a system so complex as the land law then was even the best conveyancers are not infallible. The eighteenth century law reports show that landowners frequently suffered unpleasant surprises.

Real property law has received its share of praise –

> Its merits have begun to stand out, and I hope to convince you a little later on in this lecture that it is not only one of the finest parts of our law, but that in its main principles and structure it is superior to all foreign laws dealing with this subject

says Lawson[3] – yet when we look for defects in it as it was before the legislation of 1925 the danger is of academic over-kill. Two quotations will make this clear.

> In its origin this system was eminently suitable for a society that was based and centred on the land, and appropriate to the simple notions prevailing in a feudal population, but in several respects it gradually came to outlive the reason for its existence. It tended

to become static. Rules that were in harmony with their early environment lived on long after they had become anachronisms. Law will wither unless it expands to keep pace with the progressive ideas of an advancing community, but in this particular context the rigidity and formalism of the common lawyers retarded the process, and, though equity intervened to great effect in several directions, the few reforms attempted by the legislation before the first quarter of the nineteenth century served to complicate rather than to simplify the law. Statutory reform, however, began in earnest after the report of the Real Property Commissioners in 1829. Though lavishing, as we have seen, extravagant praise upon the substantive rules of law, the commissioners went on to express their opinion that the modes by which interests in land were created, transferred and secured had become unnecessarily defective and that they demanded substantial alteration. The result of this view was that on their recommendation a number of statutes were passed between 1833 and 1837 which swept away many impediments to the smooth operation of the law.[4]

The English law of real property has never achieved that simplicity which, according to Lord Bryce, distinguishes the laws of the more civilised ages. Cromwell, in blunter style, is alleged to have called it 'a tortuous and ungodly jumble'. Its reputation has not wholly been redeemed by the reforming legislation of modern times; but it can at least be said that the path of the student is much smoother today than it was a century ago. Until about 1880 it was almost obligatory to begin any discourse on this branch of the law with apologies for many rules both intricate and uncouth. A great authority, Joshua Williams, lectured in 1878 with this preface: 'Some of the most remarkable of these laws, viewed by themselves, apart from their history, and judged only by the benefits which now result from them, appear to me to be absolutely worthless. Others are more than worthless, they are absurd and injurious.' 'Now', said Maitland, 'when those who are set to teach the youth hold such language as this, there are but two courses open to us – to silence the professors, or to reform the laws.'[5]

Nonetheless, given the importance of real property in English law plus the fact that historically it is probably the best example anywhere of law being out of step with society we must consider some aspects, and tenure above all.

English feudalism applied the doctrine of land tenure to every holder of land, no matter what duties, military or non-military, he agreed to perform. The ultimate feudal superior was the King but until the statute *Quia Emptores* of 1290 subinfeudation – the creation of sub-tenancies – was possible. There was not one kind of tenure but several, and the first division may be into free tenure and non-free tenure. Free tenure in turn may first be divided into spiritual tenure and lay tenure.

Spiritual tenures are divine services and frankalmoign. Tenure by divine services occurred where the holding was subject to specified spiritual services. It was of less importance than frankalmoign which was created when lands were granted to an ecclesiastical body on the implied understanding that it would say prayers for the repose of the soul of the granter. It is doubtful whether other feudal services could be demanded. Since after *Quia Emptores* of 1290 there could be no new grant of frankalmoign unless by the Crown, and since on alienation of the land even to another ecclesiastical body the tenure became the lay tenure known as socage, frankalmoign became uncommon. The Tenures Abolition Act of 1660 abolished knight service in s.1; and in s.7 declared that nothing in s.1 was to affect frankalmoign. The second Schedule of the Administration of Estates Act 1925 repealed s.7 of the Act of 1660. The effect of this Schedule on frankalmoign is disputed. It has been claimed[6] that the repeal is fruitless since, even if s.7 had been omitted from the 1660 Act frankalmoign would not have been affected by s.1 which abolished knight service. Others[7] argue that the effect of the Schedule is to encompass the destruction of frankalmoign. Whatever the effect of the Schedule it is clear that even long before 1925, frankalmoign had become very rare. The prime consequence of its continued existence was to complicate the law.

Free lay tenure has first to be subdivided into knight service, Sergeanty and socage (with various customary methods of land holding).

After the Norman conquest, almost all of the men who held land directly from the King held it by knight service. Each of them had to provide a fixed number of fully armed horsemen for forty days per year. For about a century the cavalry was actually recruited in this way but forty days' service per year was not a satisfactory way of running an army, so eventually money payments called scutage were substituted. By the early fourteenth century scutage had ceased to be useful for paying for the army. Apparently fewer than fifty scutages are known ever to have been levied, the last in the reign of Edward III.[8] But knight service continued because the lord from whom the land was held was entitled to certain valuable – non-military – feudal incidents, and subinfeudation could be used to exploit these. We need not consider knight service in the round since it was abolished as early as 1660, though we should note in passing that since the valuable incidents were haphazard in point of time they could not be counted on for forward economic planning.[9]

Yet we should look in some detail at one topic, the law of future interests, which is a striking instance of a body of law which cannot be said to be to the advantage of any class of society, and whose peculiarities were primarily due to the desire to prevent conveyancers from defeating the profitable incidents of tenure by knight service *in capite*. Henry VIII forced through the Statute of Uses in 1536 in order to abolish the power of devise since the major feudal incidents were due only where the heir took by descent.[10] This was followed in 1540 by the compromise of the Statute of Wills, which not only restored the power of devise to a considerable extent, namely two thirds, but provided that in reckoning the third of the deceased tenant's lands of which the King was to have the wardship, land disposed of for the advancement of the tenant's wife or the preferment of his children was to be included. Thus so far as the financial aspects were concerned, the Statute of Uses was obsolete within relatively few years. Indeed, there was a risk that it might be used for making settlements which might defeat the King's rights.

One device to that end was the life estate with remainders over. The landowner could not hope to make a family settlement which would defeat the King's claims on his own death, but if he settled his land on his eldest son for life, with remainder to the son's eldest son, the land on his son's death would not pass either by descent, or under any conveyance made by the son, and would be out of the statute. The effect of settlements of this kind remained a very moot question until late in the reign of Elizabeth I. When litigation began over the settlement which came in issue in *Chudleigh's Case*, the Queen induced the parties to agree, because of the unfortunate effects which, so her advisers warned her, a judicial decision might have upon her rights. This has escaped notice, since there is no report of the first action in print. Why the agreement broke down we do not know, but when the second action was brought[11] it was held that if a use be limited to a person unborn at the date of the conveyance, and before the cestuy que use is born the tenant under a prior limitation makes a tortious feoffment, the contingent use will be destroyed. The effect of the feoffment is to divest the estates passing under the original limitation, and unless they are re-vested by entry there will be no seisin out of which the contingent use can be executed. In this case there can be no re-entry, since the feoffor cannot re-enter against his own feoffment. In *Archer's Case*,[12] a little later, it was held that a tortious feoffment would also destroy a common law remainder limited to a person unborn. Effectively speaking, therefore, any limitation to a person unborn after a particular estate to a living person was in the power of the tenant of the freehold. This was still the law when Blackstone was writing, but various methods had been devised to avoid its effects. The most popular was to interpose, after the limitation to the first beneficiary for his life, a remainder to trustees for his life on trust for him, and to support contingent remainders, which would take effect if his estate determined in his life-time. Another was to give the first beneficiary a term of years determinable on life. Both of these devices had their hazards. Trustees to preserve contingent remainders might be omitted where they were needed. A settlement which began with a limitation for years rather than for life might fall to the ground altogether because it placed the freehold in nobody. For us, the striking fact is that the most ordinary and straighforward eighteenth century family settlement could not be effectually made unless the draftsman resorted to one or other of these devices, and this remained the law until the following century. The rule that the feoffment of a particular tenant would destroy contingent limitations dependent on his estate served only as a trap for the unwary. Its survival is an interesting illustration of the fact already remarked upon, that if a rule of law be not actually intolerable to the governing classes of a particular society, this is not in itself a proof that the rule is suited to their needs, or indeed to the needs of anyone else.

(The difficulties which might be found in understanding the preceding paragraph should not be blamed primarily on the technical terms. These terms are, I believe, sufficiently self-explanatory in the context and to define them would add to the confusion. What makes the paragraph difficult is primarily the extreme technicality of the law.)

The most interesting feature of tenure by knight's service for us is the manner in which its effects survived it. Likewise, there are many other rules of the classical English land law which can only be understood if we bear in mind that there was a time when the preservation of feudal incidents was an important object of policy. At the other end of the social scale, as we shall see, the incidents of copyhold tenure remained very much a reality until the present century.

To return to other forms of free tenure. Sergeanty, about which little need be said here, was a tenure whereby the land was held in return for services of a personal nature; and in the fourteenth century it was established that sergeanties could exist only as tenure in chief to the king. Holdings in return for particularly honourable services such as carrying the King's sword at his coronation came to be called grand sergeanty, while those for lesser military services were petit sergeanty. By the fifteenth century petit sergeanty was very much the same as socage.[13]

Socage came to be the great residual class of free tenure – though in its customs it varied from place to place – and it can reasonably be claimed to be the only one still in existence.[14] But I cannot refrain from quoting E. Jenks:[15]

> The position which will be occupied by the tenures or varieties of petit sergeanty, burgage and gavelkind after the Property legislation of 1925 takes effect is almost metaphysical in its subtlety. On the one hand, all the peculiar services of petit sergeanty are preserved by s.136 of the Law of Property Act, 1925: while all peculiar rules of descent and survivorship (the only practical importance of burgage and gavelkind) are abolished by s.45(1)(a) of the Administration of Estates Act, 1925. On the other hand, these latter tenures themselves appear not to have been expressly abolished; and the problem remains, whether a tenure which has been deprived of its only distinguishing features, can be said to have an independent existence.

As the passage shows, there were other ways of holding land apart from the regular tenures.

Gavelkind denotes the customs which applied to socage land in Kent from the Norman conquest onwards. All Kentish lands were presumed to be subject to gavelkind, but gavelkind could also exist elsewhere. In Kent the main particular rules of gavelkind were that on intestacy the land descended to all the sons equally, at the age of 15 the tenant could alienate his land by a particular form of conveyance, normally the land was devisable, the estate did not escheat in the event of attainder and execution, both the widow's dower and the widower's curtesy extended to one half of the land until remarriage, and the birth of a child was not needed for the claim of curtesy. When land outside Kent – for instance in Wales or Ireland – was shown to be subject to gavelkind this established descent of the land to all the sons but did not even create a presumption that the other peculiarities also applied.[16]

Burgage was a kind of town socage, and land held in burgage was subject to a great variety of customs. The best known form of burgage is that called borough-english which was to be found in many parts of England, particularly Sussex and Surrey, and its most striking feature was that on intestacy land descended to the youngest son.[17]

Land in ancient demesne deserves mention even though it does not fit neatly into the categories of mediaeval land law, and there is difficulty in deciding whether the tenants were freeholders or holders in villeinage.[18] These tenants were those who held land in manors which were Crown land in 1066. (Domesday Book was the only proof allowed of the status of a manor.) They could not bring the ordinary real actions, but had available special writs.

The main effect of all these forms of free tenure was to render the law much more cumbrous and complex to the advantage of no one in particular.

Unfree tenure was villeinage, which eventually gave way to copyhold which existed until it was abolished by the 1925 legislation. In its developed form it was tenure by copy of court roll at the will of the lord of the manor in which the land was situated. Copyhold land was not governed by the common law but by the customs of that particular manor – and there was great diversity of customs from one manor to another – and this continued to be so even when the common law courts took jurisdiction over copyhold customs in the sixteenth century. The courts, indeed, would refuse to enforce a copyhold custom only when it was so contrary to common sense as to be manifestly 'unreasonable'.[19]

Conveyance of copyhold was not by the ordinary deed but by 'surrender and admittance'. The tenant came to the steward in court or – where the custom permitted – out of court and, by delivering up a symbol (established by custom), resigned all his title and interest in the estate to the lord, so that the lord could grant the estate to the person who was named in the surrender. The lord was thus able to exact all the fees etc. which were inevitably due when copyhold changed hands. Cheshire rightly asserts that these payments – in effect an irregular and rather arbitrary form of private taxation – were unsatisfactory both to lord and tenant.[20] Of the various features of copyhold which were recognised as unfortunate long before 1925 only the most important need here be mentioned. Thus, the relations between lord and tenant were regulated by the immemorial customs of the manor, which could not be altered by either one of them or even by both together. An attempt by the copyholder at a direct or common law conveyance of his estate caused him to forfeit it. Unless there was an express custom to the contrary, no copyholder might commit any form of 'waste', for instance, cut timber, dig for minerals, pull down buildings or change the method of cultivation.[21] But although these timber and mineral rights were vested in the lord they were in the possession of the tenant, and for the owner to enter to take them without the tenant's consent was a trespass.[22]

Until 1925 much of England was held by copyhold tenure. The last word on the subject should be given to Cheshire:[23]

> The tenure was distinguished by several defects. For instance, the customs, which represented the local law governing land of this tenure, varied considerably from manor to manor, so that it was impossible to determine the law applicable to a disputed matter without an examination of the manorial records; the form of conveyance was far different from that required in the case of socage; copyhold and socage lands were often intermixed in so confusing a fashion as to make it difficult to discriminate between them, a dilemma from which the only escape in the event of a sale was the execution of two conveyances, one appropriate for copyhold, the other for a socage holding; certain rights of the land were so burdensome to the tenant that they caused strife and ill-will; and finally, it was impossible for either the lord or the tenant, without the assent of the other, to exploit the minerals under the land.
>
> This bare summary of the history of copyhold tenure should be enough to show that from about the beginning of the seventeenth century it was nothing more nor less than an outmoded and exceedingly inconvenient form of ordinary tenure. It served no particular social need and it certainly impeded a simplified system of conveyancing because of its frequent diversity from socage tenure. It has been rightly described as 'an anachronism and a nuisance'.

After all this, it is hardly necessary to say expressly that land tenure in England was very unsatisfactory until 1925, and that in many ways the whole structure – as it existed at various times – was out of step with the needs of society, and had been out of step for centuries.

To avoid the impression of special pleading I have in discussing the defects in tenures preferred to rely largely – too largely perhaps – on quotations from specialists on English land law. The same course will be followed in the other topic which I would like to discuss in this chapter, registration of title, that is where each land-owner's title is noted in a register which is kept up to date by marking in it all subsequent dealings which affect the land. Cheshire relates:

> So long as third parties can in this way have legally enforceable rights against land which outwardly appears to belong absolutely

to the possessor, it is difficult, in the absence of compulsory registration of title, to devise a system under which conveyances of land can be conducted with the facility of sales of goods, and it will always be incumbent on a purchaser to make careful searches and inquiries in order to see that the land is unburdened.

We may start, then, with the assumption that no effort of legislative genius can, from the point of view of simplicity and rapidity, put conveyances of land on an equal footing with sales of goods. But when the question of reforming the law came before Parliament in 1922, the result of 600 years of development from a feudal origin was that the law of real property contained so many antiquated rules and useless technicalities that additional and unnecessary impediments had arisen to hinder the facile transfer of land. The real property law as it existed in 1922 might justly be described as an archaic feudalistic system which, though originally evolved to satisfy the needs of a society based and centred on the land, had by considerable ingenuity been twisted and distorted into a shape more or less suitable to a commercial society dominated by money. The movement of progressive societies has been from land to money, or rather to trade, and a legal system which acquired its main features at a time when land constituted the major part of the country's wealth can scarcely be described as suitable to an industrial community. To borrow the words of Bagehot directed to a different subject, the 1922 real property law might be likened to 'an old man who still wears with attached fondness clothes in the fashion of his youth; what you see of him is the same; what you do not see is wholly altered'.

To take any structure, whether it be a system of law, a constitution or a house, and for a period of 600 years to patch it here and there in order to adapt it to new conditions, cannot fail to lead to complications of a bewildering character.[24]

In the first sentence of that quotation the words 'in the absence of compulsory registration of title' should be underlined. Once a system is adopted of compulsory registration of title and of encumbrances many difficulties disappear. The merest glance at the provisions in modern German law will make this plain.[25] Yet even at the present moment England does not have a system of complete registration.

The idea of registration was not unknown to the English – indeed, they introduced it into Ireland and into many colonies. At home, Henry VIII in 1535 had a bill prepared for a compulsory register of conveyances but did not succeed in having it passed.[26]

Further unsuccessful attempts were made under Cromwell and later, though in the early eighteenth century registers were set up for Middlesex and Yorkshire (but not the city of York).[27] The first report in 1829 of the Real Property Commissioners, which has already been mentioned, also suggested that what the Commissioners saw as the main defects of the system, the expense and uncertainly of titles, could best be remedied by a system of registration of titles or of assurances. Lord Westbury's Act of 1862 introduced general voluntary registration of titles but the Act failed in its purpose since the examination which was required before registration was too strict; since it was known that many titles contained deficiencies landowners preferred not to use the Act.[28] A further failure was Lord Cairns' Act of 1875 which permitted the voluntary registration of mere possessory title. Next came the Land Transfer Act 1897 which did introduce compulsory registration (and also introduced a compensation fund for persons who suffered through a mistake on the register). But registration was not enforced on the whole country and in fact was immediately compulsory only in the County of London. Upon local request, the system was to be extended to any part of the country. No such request was made before the 1925 legislation set up a new system.[29]

The 1925 legislation improved the position in two ways. First it reduced the category of legal estates and legal third party rights so that most of the latter became equitable, and it made the legal estate the basis of conveyancing. It extended the system whereby on a conveyance of the legal estate equitable third party rights were overreached so that the purchase price rather than the land itself was burdened with their payment. These equitable rights are cleared off the land if they can be satisfied from the purchase price; where they cannot be so satisfied they can be registered as land charges in a public register, thus warning purchasers and protecting their owners. If the charge is not registered it is void against a purchaser for value.[30]

Secondly the Land Registration Act 1925 s.20 provided a system of registration of title which could be extended compulsorily to any county in England or Wales by an Order in Council. Moreover land anywhere in England or Wales could be placed on the register at the owner's consent. The compulsory registration by counties proceeded very slowly, and by the Land Registration Act 1966 s.1(2) the practice of voluntary registration was suspended, the intention being to press ahead with the compulsory registration of title in all built-up areas.[31] On June 12, 1975 the Chief Land Registrar, T. B. F. Ruoff, could announce 'Thus, at last, compulsory registration for the whole of England and Wales is in sight'.[32]

If one were to ask why the system of tenure was allowed to remain so long out of step with society, and why registration – practised for centuries in Scotland and South Africa – has come in so slowly in England, one would probably receive a complex reply. In the first place, the work involved in the simplification and especially in the registration is enormous and expensive. Once a system of title to land and of conveyancing is established, it is a daunting task to introduce a new system which will apply throughout. The very complexities which contributed to make the existing system so cumbrous would be a barrier to reform. It is not a matter for surprise that a very new country, as New Zealand then was, could by ordinance of the Legislative Council in 1842 adopt many of the proposals of the English Real Property Commissioners' Report of 1829 though they were neglected at home. Secondly, human lethargy on the part of the people who suffered most and the feeling that substantial reform would not occur no doubt played an important role. Many people at times in their lives would suffer at least financially from the existing system especially when they had to pay the conveyancing fee, and many would complain loudly. Yet once the particular matter was settled they would not usually feel a permanent sense of pain, and hence they would not keep up strong, continuous pressure for reform. Thirdly, lawyers could not be expected to press for reform. Conveyancing represented (and represents) such a large proportion of their work (especially for solicitors) that they could not greet with enthusiasm any plan which would make it more difficult to justify their fees.[33] Moreover, lawyers enjoy their own technicalities. In addition, such extensive reform as was needed could come only from legislation, and English lawyers traditionally have been suspicious of statute: the quotation from Blackstone with which I began this chapter illustrates this point.

Near the beginning of this chapter we saw Lawson praising English land law both as one of the finest parts of English law and in comparison with foreign land law. The good qualities of the English law of real property should not be ignored but at least before 1925 they were not to be found in tenure or in the registration of deeds. English land law is indeed a fascinating subject; and its elaboration has been a truly remarkable feat of technical virtuosity. It is natural that a lawyer should derive pleasure from the contemplation of an excellent piece of applied legal technique. But a body of law which is technically satisfying is not for that reason alone suited to the needs of society. Its technical beauty may, and in this instance does, in part reside in the extraordinary ingenuity with which rules which on the face of it are grotesquely unsuitable have been twisted to produce a result which is or was just barely tolerable.

Notes

1. To be found in §1 of the first book of his *Commentaries on the Laws of England.*
2. See, e.g. F. H. Lawson, *The Rational Strength of English Law* (London, Stevens, 1951), p. 75.
3. *Rational Strength,* p. 76. The First Report (p. 6) of the Real Property Commissioners of 1829 claimed that English land law 'appears to come almost as near to perfection as can be expected in any human institution'.
4. *Cheshire's Modern Law of Real Property,* 11th edit. by E. H. Burn (London, Butterworth, 1972), pp. 4–5.
5. R. E. Megarry and H. W. R. Wade, *The Law of Real Property,* 3rd edit. (London, Stevens, 1966), p. 1.
6. *Cheshire's Modern Real Property,* p. 85; cf. A. W. B. Simpson, *Introduction to the History of the Land Law* (Oxford, Oxford University Press, 1961), p. 10.
7. Megarry & Wade, *Real Property,* p. 35, n. 83.
8. See Simpson, *Introduction,* p. 8.
9. Wardship was probably the most valuable, and it deserves specific mention. It was above all the lord's right to manage lands for his own profit where the tenant (as a result of succession) was a male under 21 or a female under 14 (or under 16 if not married before the land devolved to her). These rights could be sold.
10. See above all, E. W. Ives, 'The genesis of the Statute of Uses', *English Historical Review* 325 (1967), pp. 673ff.
11. (1595) 1 Co. Rep. 113b.
12. (1597) 1 Co. Rep. 63b.
13. See, e.g. *Cheshire's Modern Real Property,* pp. 19f; Simpson, *Introduction,* pp. 9f.
14. See, e.g. *Cheshire's Modern Real Property,* pp. 26f; Megarry & Wade, *Real Property,* p. 35.
15. In his (18th edition) of *Stephen's Commentaries on the Laws of England* 2 (London, Butterworth, 1925), pp. 32f.
16. See, e.g. Jenks, *Stephen's Commentaries,* p. 32; Megarry & Wade, *Real Property,* pp. 20f.
17. See, e.g. Megarry & Wade, *Real Property,* p. 22.
18. See, e.g. Simpson, *Introduction,* pp. 155f.
19. See G. C. Cheshire's edition (19th) of *Stephen's Commentaries on the Laws of England* 2 (London, Butterworth, 1928), pp. 46f.
20. *Stephen's Commentaries* 2, p. 47.
21. E. Jenks, *Stephen's Commentaries* 2, pp. 40f. Jenks also describes the curious way in which disputes to copyhold title were decided.

22. See Megarry & Wade, *Real Property*, p. 29.

23. *Modern Real Property*, p. 26.

24. *Modern Real Property*, pp. 6f.

25. See, e.g. Palandt, *Bürgerliches Gesetzbuch*, 33rd edit. by various authors (Munich, Beck, 1974), pp. 994ff; E. J. Cohn, *Manual of German Law* 1, 2nd edit. (London, British Institute of International and Comparative Law, 1968), pp. 186ff.

26. See, e.g. C. D'O. Farran, *Principles of Scots and English Land Law* (Edinburgh, Green, 1958), p. 213; Simpson, *Introduction*, p. 254.

27. See Cheshire, *Stephen's Commentaries* 2, pp. 445f; The Middlesex Deeds Registry was abolished by the Land Registration Act, 1936; those of Yorkshire by the Law of Property Act, 1967, ss. 16–22.

28. See Simpson, *loc. cit.*

29. Simpson, *Introduction*, p. 255. A significant fact is, of course, that first registration can be very expensive. Moreover, without the curtain registration is not practicable.

30. For this paragraph see Law of Property Act 1925, s. 1; Settled Land Act 1925, s. 4; Land Charges Act 1925; *Cheshire's Modern Real Property*, pp. 93ff. Mr. John Barton kindly tells me that in his view it is very arguable that the 1925 legislation itself is more appropriate to the 19th century than to this.

31. See for further detail *Cheshire's Modern Real Property*, pp. 102ff.

32. *Report to the Lord Chancellor on H.M. Land Registry for the Year 1974–1975* (London, H.M.S.O., 1975), p. 3.

33. See, e.g. Farran, *Principles*, pp. 216ff.

Chapter 6

ENGLISH LAW:
LIBEL AND SLANDER

The significance of the law of defamation is well stressed by E. C. S. Wade:

> Defamation is the branch of the common law which closely affects what is perhaps the most important of the political freedoms, that of speech and criticism. Its operation at all times affects the existence of a free press.[1]

English law draws a distinction in defamation which seems to be unknown to systems not founded on the Common Law; a defamatory statement is libel if it is cast in a form which is not purely transitory, but slander if oral (and unrecorded) words or gestures. Naturally it is not always easy to distinguish. P. F. Carter-Ruck thinks that the keenest example of a borderline case would be smoke signwriting from an aeroplane.[2] The Faulks Committee reporting in 1975 suggests that defamatory sky-writing would be libel because the vapour takes some little time to disperse.[3] The practical difference between libel and slander is that the former is actionable *per se*, the latter – unless it falls within a particular exceptional category – is not actionable unless financial loss has actually been suffered.

The Faulks Committee recommend the abolition of the distinction and it is worth quoting the first paragraph of their conclusions.[4]

> The distinction between libel and slander is entirely attributable to historical accident, but for which it would never have come into being. It represents one of the few spheres (if not the only one) in which the forms of action continue to rule us from the grave. It renders this part of the law unreasonable and unnecessarily complicated and refined, carrying a host of rules and exceptions, derived partly from precedent and partly from statute, which are illogical, difficult to learn, and in certain applications, it must be added, unjust. To an outsider, at least, it appears contrary to normal concepts of justice that a personal enemy might with

impunity carry on a deliberate and malicious campaign of oral vilification relating, let us say, to the sexual habits of a person who does not have a profession, calling, trade or business in which the campaign would be likely to injure him. Further, it would be impossible for the victim, being unable to aver and prove actual pecuniary loss, even to obtain an injunction to stop the campaign. On the other hand, if the loss of one dinner invitation could be proved, the victim could recover substantial and even punitive damages. If in the case of libel the plaintiff may be awarded such damages as will 'compensate him for the distress, humiliation and annoyance which the libel has caused him', irrespective of any proof of actual pecuniary loss, it seems wholly unreasonable that the same should not be true of slander.

That quotation has a particular interest for us even apart from the immediate topic. It reveals the belief of the members of the Committee that defamation is exceptional in being an archaic survival, out-of-step with society's needs. Experts in other fields also seem to believe that their speciality is unusual in its power of unnecessary longevity. For instance:

In time, of course, the curtailment of the geographical mobility of labourers was no longer requisite. One might well expect that when the legal function served by the statutes was no longer an important one for the society, the statutes would be eliminated from the law. In fact this has not occurred. The vagrancy statutes have remained in effect since 1349. Furthermore, as we shall see in some detail later, they were taken over by the colonies and have remained in effect in the United States as well.[5]

And L. C. B. Gower, explaining why the English Law Commission wished to codify the law of contract, wrote:[6]

In this sphere, the common law has not, unfortunately, continued to display its customary ability to adapt itself to changing conditions. To a small extent, but to a small extent only, this has been corrected by legislative intervention, as with the Law Reform (Frustrated Contracts) Act 1943.

We need not, I think, go deeply into the historical origins of the distinction between libel and slander which was well-established by the seventeenth century.[7] The distinction seems, however, to have originated in governmental suspicion of the press. Thus, not only was the publication of a libel a crime whether it were true or false, but it was widely held in the eighteenth century that the truth of the imputation was not a defence even in an action for damages.[8] The extraordinary law of slander is primarily due to the fact that defamation was considered in the sixteenth century to be properly a matter for the ecclesiastical courts. Thus, when the action on the case for words developed, it was accepted that to sustain an action at common law it was not enough that the words were defamatory in themselves, it must also be shown that the action raised a question which was properly of temporal cognisance, either because it was one which the ecclesiastical court would not be permitted to examine (as the commission of a temporal offence) or because the imputation prejudiced the plaintiff in his trade or his estate – an ecclesiastical court could not award compensation for temporal loss.[9] The converse of this rule was that an imputation of an ecclesiastical offence was not actionable at common law – which is the reason it was necessary to show special damage if an action was brought for an imputation of unchastity. The odder elaborations of the common law categories of slander actionable *per se* are largely a consequence of the fact that these categories have survived the original reason for their existence – indeed, the reason has been forgotten.

What, of course, matters to us is that the failings of the distinction have been obvious for a long time.[10] In 1812 Sir James Mansfield, Lord Chief Justice, declared he could see no good reason why an action should lie for the written word which did not lie for the spoken.[11] In 1843 a Select Committee of the House of Lords issued a *Report on the law of defamation* which advocated the abolition of the distinction but which was never acted on. In 1902, F. Carr began an article on the distinction with the words:

If an intelligent foreigner, having an intimate acquaintance with the Legal Systems of modern Europe, were asked after *a priori* consideration to pronounce on the authenticity or otherwise of some half dozen or so main propositions in the English law of Defamation, it is safe to say that in the majority of instances his pronouncement would be wrong.

If, for example, he were to be asked whether or no he thought it possible that an English lady could in the end of the nineteenth century be assailed by spoken slander imputing the vilest forms of unchastity, without any civil remedy, whatsoever, he would not hesitate in saying 'No'. But yet, until 1891, the imputation of adultery to a married woman, however malicious and industrious the circulation of the lie, was not *per se* actionable. The Slander of Women Act, however, of that year, for us marked a very great advance. For it quickened the atrophy of centuries, and actually, in one small respect, made our law as civilized as that of the Mosaic system of more than three thousand years sooner. Still, we are conservative, and the Act did not go very far. For even now the imputation of lightness and immorality, provided that it fall short of the very carnal offence, is without remedy; and the above grudging concession to the female sex is restricted to them; and for men the ruling of *Lumby v. Allday* is still law, though a man's reputation for decency and courage is not less dear to him than her fair fame is to a woman.

To render the confusion of the intelligent foreigner under our examination yet more confounded, it is merely necessary to tell him that if the slandered woman happened to be a citizen of London or Bristol, her character might be vindicated. And that this is not due to the fact that these cities are more enlightened, but that in these municipalities it was the custom to whip the approved meretrix at the cart's tail.

If, dropping the form of interrogation, you were to tell him that the editor of a newspaper, who, in perfectly good faith, had published the incorrect but innocent statement that a certain cantatrice was the mother of a lady of like profession, had to pay the sum of two thousand pounds compensation to the alleged parent; our examinee might shrug his shoulders and tell us, 'C'est magnifique, mais ce n'est pas la raison'. But at the pro-position, that to say of a solicitor, in the presence of hundreds of people, that he had been guilty of fraud on his creditors and been whipped off a race-course, was not actionable; he might well wonderingly ask where was the boasted equality of Englishmen before the law, when there was this great difference between the respective liabilities of the libeller and slanderer. And he might equally well ask whether 'ubi jus, ibi remedium' was anything else than a mere insulting sham.[12]

And the Faulks Committee reports that since then probably no academic writer has supported the distinction and that many of the most eminent have condemned it. They list Sir William Holdsworth, Spencer Bower, Sir Frederick Pollock, Professor E. C. S. Wade and Professor Winfield.[13] The Committee itself recommends the abolition of the distinction, and the assimilation of slander to libel.[14]

Earlier the majority of the Porter Committee which reported in 1948 had favoured the retention of the distinction[15] though they declared the present law 'arbitrary and illogical'. The only argument they gave for retention was that if all slanders were made actionable *per se* 'the scope for trivial but costly litigation might be enormously increased'. As the Faulks Committee observed,[16] the evidence for the argument is not stated. The Porter Committee conceded that in Scotland the distinction was not made, and no serious disadvantages had been suffered.

We could explore further the absurdities of the distinction between libel and slander but there are many other topics in defamation which are of equal interest. We might for instance consider some of the rules relating to unintentional defamation before 1952.

For defamation the test is not what the defendant intended to mean but whether the matter complained of does 'in fact tend to lower the plaintiff in the estimation of right-thinking men or cause him to be shunned and avoided or expose him to hatred, ridicule or contempt'. A few famous examples may serve as illustration.

(1) In 1908 the *Sunday Chronicle* published an article in chatty vein on motor races at Dieppe and declared

'There is Artemus Jones with a woman who is not his wife, who must be you know – the other thing!!' whispered a fair neighbour of mine excitedly into her bosom-friend's ear.

Artemus Jones, who was intended to be a fictitious character, was further described as a churchwarden at Peckham. A barrister on the North Wales circuit had been baptised Thomas Jones and – Jones being a common name in Wales – he took his father's advice and called himself 'Thomas Artemus Jones'. Some of his friends abbreviated this to 'Artemus Jones', and under that name he had contributed articles to the *Sunday Chronicle* between 1899 and 1901. He was not a churchwarden and did not live at Peckham; nor had he been to Dieppe. But he sued the newspaper proprietors for libel and the jury awarded him £1,750 damages. The House of Lords upheld the decision.[17]

(2) A man named Cassidy who also called himself Corrigan and described himself as a General in the Mexican Army had a wife who also called herself Mrs. Cassidy or Mrs. Corrigan, at whose flat he occasionally stayed. On February 18, 1928 he was at Hurst Park races in company with a woman (described as Miss X) and he authorised a press agent to take a picture of both of them and announce their engagement. The photograph appeared in the *Daily Mirror*, with the words underneath, 'Mr. M. Corrigan, the race horse owner, and Miss "X", whose engagement has been announced.' Mrs. Cassidy sued the newspaper for defamation on the ground that since they had published the statement that Corrigan was unmarried, she must be regarded as his mistress. In the action

she was successful and the jury awarded £500 damages. The Court of Appeal upheld the verdict.[18]

(3) In the magazine *Men Only* for January 1952 appeared a picture showing a cocktail bar with the words 'Spider's Web' above it. In the picture a man smoking a large cigar was introducing a middle-aged male customer to an extravagantly made-up woman sitting at the bar, who was indecently attired in an inadequate and suggestive dress. Underneath the picture were the words 'Welcome to the Spider's Web.' The proprietors of a licensed restaurant and roadhouse at Watford By-Pass called 'The Spider's Web' sued the proprietors and publishers and the printers of the magazine, alleging that:

> by the picture and words, the defendants meant and were understood to mean that the plaintiffs caused and permitted and employed women of loose morals to frequent their premises, that male customers visiting the premises were introduced to such women by the management for immoral purposes, and that the premises were a bawdy lair and a place of resort of prostitutes, and should not be frequented or visited by any respectable person.

The defendants denied that the picture or words referred or were capable of referring to the plaintiffs, or that they bore or were capable of bearing any meaning defamatory of the plaintiffs. The defendants also claimed that neither the publishers nor the artist knew of this particular roadhouse but had chosen the name because of the nursery-rhyme, 'The Spider and the Fly'.

In the Queen's Bench Division, McNair J. accepted the claim of the defendants but held that the picture was capable of the interpretation of the plaintiffs, and that a reasonable man would so interpret it. He therefore found in favour of the plaintiffs, and declared it right that damages should not be of an extravagant but of a significant figure. He was satisfied no real harm had been done to the plaintiffs and awarded them £500 damages.[19]

In these and similar cases of unintentional defamation,[20] substantial damages – as we have seen – might be awarded. Liability, of course, did not depend on the defendant's intention, nor would he escape liability if it could be shown that he had taken due care. Not just the publisher and author, but also the printer was liable. The Porter Committee recommended[21] that for unintentional libel published despite all reasonable care being taken by the defendant, publication of a suitable correction and apology would be sufficient amends, and this was adopted in the Defamation Act, 1952, s.4.[22]

By a beautiful piece of unconscious irony, H.M.S.O. had to issue an errata slip to the Porter Committee's *Report*, part of which read 'Paragraph (4) *Unintentional Defamation*, line 3 – "aware" *should read* "unaware".'

In the light of awards of damages before 1952 for unintentional libel we should return briefly to the distinction between slander and libel. Let us imagine that at that time a person quite maliciously uttered damaging lies about another person – but not in respect of his trade – at a public meeting, and that journalists who were present published the story in all innocence. Unless the injured person could actually prove that he suffered a financial loss from the statement he had (and has) no right of action against the wicked speech-maker but he had against the journalists, publishers and printers who were acting in good faith. Indeed, even if the statement is printed so that it can be denied, those responsible for the publication are liable for defamation. This last point is well illustrated by *Breasley v. Odhams Press Ltd.*[23] a case brought in 1963 in the Queen's Bench Division by the champion jockey after he lost the Byfleet Stakes in 1961. An article in the *Daily Herald* for November 9, 1961 contained:

A small group of punters stood at the entrance of the Newbury unsaddling enclosure and bellowed insults at Scobie Breasley because he failed to win the last race yesterday. They accused Breasley of not trying after he was beaten on the odds-on favourite Indian Conquest and implied he had lost the race to benefit the bookmakers. 'Go back to Australia' they shouted in Scobie's face. . . .'Is this another for the bookmakers?' they jeered. . . . Cundall [a trainer] demanded that they all looked closely at both horses standing in the winner's enclosure where the winner Utrillo II, looked unruffled by his efforts to win the mile race while the loser sweated a great deal. Faced with such authoritative opinion, the demonstration fizzled out and it was freely admitted they were speaking through their pockets. . . . What annoyed the barrackers yesterday was the position – last of the four – that Breasley chose for Indian Conquest before he started his challenge two furlongs from the winning post. The loud-mouthed gents yesterday overlooked the similar style which Breasley has adopted on the Brighton course – over which he is the undisputed champion rider. On this and other courses he has shown himself a master of tactics and I accept his judgement. . . .

Havers, J. declared the words were capable of bearing a defamatory meaning, and the jury awarded the jockey £250 damages.

Should it be argued that in any such case the worst absurdities might be tempered by the award of minimal damages, one may make the rejoinder first that the rules of positive law should not favour absurd decisions. Secondly, one should take into account the social costs of compelling juries to sit, of providing judges and courts, and even the delays caused to other, more serious, actions. Thirdly, the award of trivial damages does nothing to alleviate the crushing burden of the defendant's own costs even if he does not have to pay those of the plaintiff. Fourthly, according to The Newspapers Mutual Insurance Society Limited,

> Libel costs a lost of money; much more than is generally realised, because for every claim that reaches court there are dozens settled between the claimants' solicitors and the newspapers' solicitors.[24]

Another subject well worth a glance is the defendant's plea in mitigation of damages that the plaintiff had a general bad reputation prior to the publication of the defamation which is the subject of the action. The law is quite clear. The defendant can only lead evidence which goes to the *general* bad reputation of the plaintiff and he is not entitled to produce evidence of particular acts of misconduct by the plaintiff which tend to show his character or disposition even though these specific acts would indicate that the plaintiff deserved an extremely bad reputation.[25] The law was settled by *Scott v. Sampson* in 1882 and was severely criticised by the Porter Committee[26] which considered that, as a pure matter of theory, the doctine propounded in *Scott v. Sampson* might be supported, but, in practice, it leads to curious and inequitable results.[27] The Committee pointed out above all that it is almost impossible to find witnesses – who would be subjected to cross-examination – prepared to give evidence that the plaintiff is of general bad reputation, no matter now bad his general reputation may be.[28] Accordingly, the Committee recommended that a defendant who gave due notice to the plaintiff should be entitled, in order to mitigate damages, to rely upon specific instances of misconduct by the plaintiff, other than those charged in the publication complained of.[29] As a result the original Defamation Bill which was presented to Parliament following upon the Porter Committee's recommendation had, as clause 11:

> In any action for libel or slander, the defendant may give evidence in mitigation of damages of any fact relevant to the character or reputation of the plaintiff not being facts charged in the words on which the action is founded.

But this clause was lost, apparently because it was not possible to put it to the House if the Third Reading was to be completed on the relevant day.[30] As we shall see from other examples also, pressure – of various kinds – on the legislature are one important reason for law being out of step with the known needs and desires of society.

The need for a reform of the type proposed by the unsuccessful clause 11 was more than amply demonstrated by *Plato Films Ltd v. Speidel* in 1961. General Hans Speidel, the Supreme Commander of Allied Land Forces in Europe, claimed damages for libel against the U.K. distributors of a film in which he was depicted as privy to the murders of King Alexander of Yugoslavia and M. Barthou in 1934, and as having betrayed Field-Marshal Rommel in June, 1944. The defendants pleaded justification and, alternatively in mitigation of damages, said that evidence would be given at the trial of (A) the circumstances under which the alleged libel was published, and (B) the plaintiff's character. They pleaded as particulars of (A) that the matters of complaint formed part of the film in which the plaintiff was further depicted as guilty of specific acts, such as the taking and/or shooting of civilian hostages, the deportation of Jews to concentration camps, being responsible for acts generally accepted among civilised peoples as being contrary to the rules of warfare, engaging in espionage while attached to the German Embassy in Paris between 1934 and 1938, the truth of which the plaintiff did not deny. Under (B) the defence pleaded that the plaintiff was widely reputed to have been and in fact was guilty inter alia of the acts specified in (A). In the Court of Appeal, Ormerod and Devlin L.JJ. held that sub-paragraph (A) should be struck out and gave leave for (B) to be amended to read:

> Alternatively in mitigation of damages the defendants will at the trial of the action give evidence in chief that the plaintiff had on or before November 19, 1958, a bad reputation as a man who was a party to and/or responsible for acts which were war crimes and/or against humanity and/or atrocities.

On appeal a very strong House of Lords – Viscount Simonds, Lord Radcliffe, Lord Denning, Lord Morris of Borth-y-Gest and Lord Guest – held (1) that sub-paragraph (A) was objectionable and should be struck out and (2) that as to sub-paragraph (B) evidence of particular acts of misconduct could not be given in mitigation of damages where the defendants had failed to justify the libel complained of. Lord Radcliffe dissented from (2). In his view it would be wrong to hold that general evidence of reputation cannot include evidence of particular incidents if they are of sufficient notoriety to be likely to contribute to the plaintiff's current reputation.

The Faulks Committee reported[31]:

The decision in *Plato Films v. Speidel* itself incurred considerable criticism both from 'Justice', the British section of the International Commission of Jurists, and from the International Press Institute, and in the Freedom of Publication Bill introduced into Parliament in 1966 there was a clause amending the law in this respect, but the Bill never reached the Statute Book.

And they recommended[32]:

that there should be admissible in mitigation of damages evidence of any matter, general or particular, relevant at the date of the trial to that aspect of the plaintiff's reputation with which the defamation is concerned. Rules of Court should provide that notice should be given of any matter on which a party intends to rely.

It is scarcely necessary, I think, to stress the limitations placed on freedom of speech as a result of the rule in *Scott v. Samspon*, or to repeat that the law was settled thus in 1882, and that the defects have been apparent for some considerable time.

A different matter which cries out for attention here is the beautiful complexity of the defence of 'fair comment' and the 'rolled up plea' especially as they existed before 1952. The scope of 'fair comment' is best described in the immortal words of Lord Esher, M.R. in 1887:

Every latitude must be given to opinion and to prejudice and then an ordinary set of men with ordinary judgement must say whether any fair man would have made such a comment. . . . Mere exaggeration, or even gross exaggeration, would not make the comment unfair. However wrong the opinion expressed may be in point of truth, or however prejudiced the writer, it may still be within the prescribed limit. The question which the jury must consider is this – 'Would any fair man, however prejudiced he may be, however exaggerated or obstinate his views, have said that which this criticism has said of the work which is criticised?'[33]

It should be added that later cases have created a minor exception: where the statement complained of imputes corrupt or dishonourable motives to the plaintiff, the defendant must establish that the statement was actually warranted by the facts.

For the defence of 'fair comment' to apply, the facts on which the comment was based must have been truly stated. As the Porter Committee explained,[34]

> in practice, the rule has been applied with a continually growing rigidity, with the result that, where the libel complained of consists in part of statements of fact and in part of expressions of opinion, the defence of 'fair comment' may fail *in limine* if one of the defamatory statements of fact contained in the alleged libel is incorrect in some minor and apparently unimportant detail.

No one would claim that this was a satisfactory state of affairs for the defendants. But the complexity is compounded and a fresh advantage given in turn to the defendant by what is known as the 'rolled-up plea', a defence plead as: 'In so far as the words complained of consist of statements of fact, they are true in substance and in fact; in so far as they consist of expression of opinion, they are fair comment made in good faith and without malice upon the said facts, which are a matter of public interest.' The beauty of this plea is that it is for the jury – or for the judge if he is sitting alone – to decide at the trial which words represent fact and which represent comment. (One should also add that it is for the judge, even sitting with a jury, to determine whether the matter commented on is one of public interest.)[35] Consequently, the defendant cannot be compelled to set out in his defence which statements he alleges were statements of fact and which he alleges were comment. Indeed, it has been held by the Court of Appeal that he cannot be indirectly compelled to specify which statements are statements of fact, by being compelled to deliver particulars of the facts relied on in support of his plea.[36] The Porter Committee rightly pointed out that this worked a manifest injustice to the plaintiff who might not know the specific allegations of fact which would be made against him.[37]

As a result of the Porter Committee's recommendations, s.6 of the Defamation Act 1952 permitted the defence of fair comment not to fail simply because every allegation of fact could not be proved, provided the expression of opinion is fair comment with regard to the alleged facts which are proved. And now the Faulks Committee *Report*[38] recommends the abolition of the 'rolled-up plea'.

As a final topic – among several possibilities – in defamation, let us consider the happy bankrupt. It is not necessary to do more than quote the appropriate section from Carter-Ruck's *Libel and Slander*:[39]

Bankrupts are in an enviable position in libel actions for the dice are loaded heavily in their favour. They have nothing to lose and everything to gain; whereas the defendant – even if he wins – knows that he must be substantially out-of-pocket, for he will not be able to recover any costs from his impecunious adversary.

A bankrupt's right of action in respect of defamation does not pass to his trustees,[40] nor can his trustees claim any damages which he recovers in such an action.[41] The trustees cannot bring an action for defamation in the name of the bankrupt, even if the defamation was the cause of the bankruptcy.[42] A libel action, therefore, offers the bankrupt an opportunity of collecting a sum of money upon which his creditors will not be able to lay their hands.

A bankrupt will not be ordered to lodge security for the defendant's costs merely because he is a plaintiff and is a bankrupt, although such an order is invariably made against a company which is in liquidation. The only thing that the defendant can do is to apply to the court for an order that the action be transferred to the County Court, unless the bankrupt lodges – by way of security for the defendant's costs – a sum of money, usually fixed at a totally inadequate figure. The court has a discretion in such an application and will be reluctant to make the order if the case is one of any magnitude. In any event the County Court machinery is not designed to deal with complicated actions for defamation and is not really a suitable tribunal for such actions. An action for defamation may be brought against a bankrupt but a successful plaintiff is not permitted to prove in the bankruptcy for the amount of his damages or costs unless he signs judgement before the making of the receiving order.[43] In practice there is little point in bringing a libel action against a bankrupt, except to prevent a repetition of the libel, unless there is a reasonable prospect that at some time in the future he may be worth something. His discharge from the bankruptcy will not operate to release him from the liability to pay the judgement in such an action.[44]

The general conclusion of this chapter scarcely needs stating. Despite its importance for the happiness of individuals and the welfare of society, the law of defamation has been and is marred by grave defects which have caused it to be inefficient and out of step with the needs and desires both of society as a whole and with any ruling élite.[45]

Notes

1. 'Defamation', *LQR* 66 (1950), pp. 348ff at p. 348.
2. *Libel and Slander* (London, Faber, 1972), p. 20.
3. *Report of the Committee on Defamation* (London, H.M.S.O., 1975), Cmnd. 5909, p. 17.
4. *Report* §86, p. 20.
5. W. Chambliss, 'Vagrancy Law in England and America', *Social Problems* 12 (1964), pp. 67ff; reprinted in D. Black & M. Mileski, *The Social Organization of Law* (New York, London, Seminar Press, 1973), pp. 132ff at p. 136.
6. *MLR* 30 (1967), p. 259. The Commission has now abandoned the idea of codifying the law of contract *in toto*.
7. See Carter-Ruck, *Libel and Slander*, pp. 37ff; *Report*, Appendix VI, p. 258.
8. See R. Woddeson, *A Systematical View of the Law of England* 3 (London, 1792), pp. 177ff.
9. See the prophetic observations in the *New Additions* of St. German, *Doctor and Student* edit. by T. F. T. Plucknett and J. L. Barton (London, Seldon Society, 1974), pp. 330f.
10. See the Faulks Report, pp. 18ff.
11. *Thorley v. Kerry* (1812) 4 Taunt. 355.
12. 'The English Law of Defamation: with especial Reference to the Distinction between Libel and Slander', *LQR* 18 (1902), pp. 255ff.
13. §82, p. 19. The references given to the academic writers are, in order: *History of English Law* 8, p. 378; *Actionable Defamation*, 2nd ed. 1923, pp. 286–289; 66 *LQR*, p. 348; *Tort*, 5th edit., pp. 247, 255.
14. §91, p. 21.
15. *Report of the Committee on the Law of Defamation* (London, H.M.S.O., 1948), Cmd. 7536, §§36–40, pp. 12f.
16. §85, p. 19.
17. *Hulton & Co. Ltd. v. Jones* (1910) A.C. 20 (H.L.). It has been suggested that the decision was based on recklessness or even spite; Salmond, *Law of Torts*, 16th edit. by R. F. V. Heuston (London, Sweet & Maxwell, 1973), p. 146, no. 60.
18. *Cassidy v. Daily Mirror Newspapers Ltd.* [1929] 2 K.B. 331; see also *Ralston v. Ralston* [1930] 2 K.B. 238.
19. *The Times*, April 17, 18, 1953.
20. See, e.g. *Newstead v. London Express Newspaper Ltd.* (1940) 1 K.B. 377 (though in that case damages were assessed at one farthing); *Hough v. London Express Newspaper Ltd.* (1940), 2 K.B. 507; *Capital and Counties Bank Ltd. v. Henty* (1882) 7 A.C. 741; *Lewis v. Daily Telegraph Ltd.* (1963) 2 All E.R. 151; *Morgan v. Odhams Press Ltd.* (1971) 2 All E.R. 1156. For instances of absurd decisions in other areas of Anglo-American law see, e.g. O. Kahn-Freund, 'English Law and American Law – Some Comparative Reflections',

in *Essays in Jurisprudence in Honor of Roscoe Pound* edit. by R. A. Newman (Indianapolis, Bobbs-Merrill, 1962), pp. 362ff; E. H. Levi, *Introduction to Legal Reasoning* (Chicago, University of Chicago Press, 1948).

21. §§62–73.
22. For the effect of the section see Carter-Ruck, *Libel and Slander*, pp. 164ff; Gatley, *Libel and Slander*, pp. 810ff.
23. *The Times*, Nov. 13, 14, 15, 1963.
24. *A Second Look at Libel* (The Newspaper Mutual Insurance Society Ltd., 1971), p. 6.
25. *Scott v. Sampson* (1882) 8 Q.B.D. 491; *Hobbs v. Tinling & Co. Ltd.* [1929] 2 K.B.1; *Plato Films v. Speidel* [1961] A.C. 1090.
26. *Report*, §§1146–156, pp. 35ff.
27. §148.
28. §149.
29. §156. See also the fate of the Domicile Bills of the 1950's; A. V. Dicey and J. H. C. Morris, *The Conflict of Laws*, 9th edit. by Morris and others (London, Stevens, 1973), pp. 126ff; M. Mann, 'The Domicile Bills' 8 *I.C.L.Q.* (1959), pp. 457ff.
30. Evidence of H. A. Taylor, past President of the Institute of Journalists and a member of the Porter Committee, to the Faulks Committee; *Report* §368, p. 102.
31. §368, p. 102.
32. §372, p. 103.
33. *Merivale v. Carson* (1887) 20 Q.B.D. 275 at 280f. Lord Porter would prefer to substitute 'honest' for 'fair'; *Turner v. M.G.M. Pictures Ltd.* [1950] 1 All E.R. 449 at 461.
34. *Report* §87, p. 22.
35. The subject is even more complex! See Gatley, *Libel and Slander*, pp. 750ff and the cases referred to.
36. See for this the Porter Committee *Report*, §174, p. 40.
37. *Report*, §175, pp. 40f.
38. §176, p. 45.
39. Pp. 85f. The footnote references which follow are numbered in accordance with this chapter. In Carter-Ruck they run from 11 to 15.
40. *Benson v. Flower* (1630) W. Jones 215.
41. Ex. p. Vine (1878) 8 Ch.D. 364, C.A.
42. Per Alderson, B. in *Howard v. Crowther* (1841) 8 M. & W. at p. 604, 151 E.R. at p. 1180.
43. Ex. p. Brooke (1876) 3 Ch.D. 494, C.A.
44. Bankruptcy Act, 1914, Section 30 (1), 4 and 5 Geo. 5 c. 59.
45. We have not considered in this chapter those cases which in the history of defamation have proceeded on the basis of absurd argument to what might possibly be thought a wholesome result. Foremost among these are the early cases decided with the intention of discouraging the bringing of actions. An interesting example is in the

report of the case of Sir Thomas Holt (1608) Cro. Jac. 184 which is quoted in Carter-Ruck, *Libel and Slander*, p. 40. On the general feeling of *malaise* over the law of defamation, see the preface to Gatley, *Libel and Slander*.

Chapter 7

WIDER PERSPECTIVES

It is, in fact, much easier to make out the case that English law to a marked extent is, and has been, out of step with its society than it is for Roman law. It may be thought that in the preceding two chapters I have made things too simple for myself by choosing notorious examples. In a sense the charge is just, but it is in the nature of things for this work to choose obvious and non-controversial examples. If one wants to demonstrate that rules of law do not jibe with the wishes or needs of society and its leaders, then one has to show that society or at least its lawyers are well aware of the law's defects. And when one deals with existing rules or those recently abolished as in English law, this of necessity involves taking instances which are very obvious, and showing that they are notorious.

What is interesting, though, is that the English examples are more notorious than those from Roman law. I would attribute this in the first place to historical circumstances which made criticism of legal rules in ancient Rome less frequent, then to historical factors which would reduce the survival rate of legal criticism.[1] More important, however, was the later traditional respect in which Roman law was held – for instance in the Age of Reason Roman law (with slight modifications) was regarded as the Law of Reason – and its position as a system not in vigour – or at the very least not entirely so – which meant that lawyers were more concerned with discovering what the rules were than with determining how well they worked. It has perhaps been an advantage for the reputation of Roman law as a system that for a period of about five centuries after its codification by Justinian it was out of use and in effect unknown in the West, that it did not suffer a gradual decline but (in the form known to us) was almost totally eclipsed, only to be rediscovered as part of a general renaissance. It is, of course, impossible to determine whether Roman law or English law was less out of harmony with its society. No test exists which could measure this. Nor could one determine which period of time for each system should be chosen for a just comparison.

So far as English law is concerned it would have been equally possible to choose other areas in which in the recent past (and even in the present) absurdities abounded. Perhaps, despite the thrust of this book, it would be an advantage to show that private law is not the only branch which can be badly out of step with the needs and desires of society, hence I will say a word or two about a few aspects of criminal law.

First, the distinction between felonies and misdemeanours, which was abolished by s.1 of the Criminal Law Act 1967. The former were those crimes which before the Forfeiture Act 1870 involved forfeiture of the convicted person's goods and land, and crimes which were declared by statute to be felonies. The latter were all crimes which were not felonies or treasons.[2] Though this is perhaps the best way to distinguish felonies and misdemeanours it is not wholly satisfactory. Thus misprison of treason (i.e. the failure to disclose treason to the police) was only a misdemeanour yet did involve forfeiture. But to say that a felony was a crime punishable by death would not meet the case; petty larceny, a felony, was never punishable by death: piracy which was punishable by death was never a felony.[3] Originally felonies were the crimes created by the common law which dealt only with serious crimes, and it would be a fair generalisation to say that once upon a time felonies were the crimes which were regarded as more serious, misdemeanours as less serious, but this long ago ceased to be anything like absolutely true. In 1883 Sir James Fitzjames Stephen described the distinction as 'unmeaning and a source of confusion'[4] as a result of the restrictions on the death penalty and the abolition of benefit of clergy. Yet the distinction survived. In the 1960's, bigamy was a felony punishable by up to seven years' imprisonment; fraudulent conversion and perjury were both only misdemeanours but could also carry a sentence of seven years' imprisonment. Simple larceny was a felony punishable by up to five years' imprisonment, obtaining by false pretences was a misdemeanour which carried the possibility of the same penalty. Forgery was only a misdemeanour until the Forgery Act 1913. By the Bankruptcy Act 1914, s.159 it was a felony for a bankrupt to leave England taking more than £20 of his property with him, but the maximum penalty was two years imprisonment.

The distinction would have been 'unmeaning' but not much worse were it not that whether a crime was a felony or a misdemeanour had important consequences. Thus, for instance, if a felon resisted arrest or attempted to flee and he could not otherwise be brought or kept in custody, he could lawfully be killed.[5] A person who committed a misdemeanour and was escaping could not be killed. Again, a private person could arrest another without a warrant if the latter had committed a felony or dangerous breach of the peace in his presence; or if he reasonably suspected the latter of committing a felony which actually had been committed by someone;[6] or if he was expressly authorised by statute to arrest without a warrant. In addition and of greater practical importance a police constable could also arrest without a warrant a person whom he reasonably suspected of having committed a felony whether or not a felony actually was committed.[7] In other cases, notably involving misdemeanours, arrest without a warrant was unlawful. (The present position is that where an arrestable offence – defined by the Criminal Law Act 1967 s.2 as an offence 'for which the sentence is fixed by law or for which a person (not previously convicted) may under or by virtue of any enactment be sentenced for a term of five years, and to attempt to commit any such offence' – has been committed any person may arrest without warrant a person who is guilty or whom he has reasonable cause to suspect is guilty.) Further the injured person could not bring civil proceedings against a felon until he had been prosecuted, or a reasonable cause for the failure to prosecute him had been shown.[8] Only in felonies was a distinction drawn between principals and accessories. A person who for a felony would have been an accessory before the fact was a principal for a misdemeanour or treason; an accessory after the fact for a felony would be a principal in a treason, and not involved in the crime for a misdemeanour.[9] The Forfeiture Act 1870 s.4 gave the court power, upon conviction for felony, to award the injured party up to £100 in respect of loss of property. By s.2 of the same Act, a person convicted of felony for which he was sentenced to death or not less than 12 months imprisonment was for the duration of his sentence disqualified from holding public office, sitting in Parliament and voting in elections. A pension ceased to be payable (but by s.70(2) of the Criminal Justice Act 1948 the authority paying the pension had discretion to restore it). These disqualifications did not apply to a misdemeanant though he might be expelled from Parliament. Finally (for our purposes), misprision, i.e. concealment, of a felony was a misdemeanour, though misprision of a misdemeanour was no offence; compounding, i.e. agreeing not to prosecute, a felony was a crime, but, generally, compounding a misdemeanour was not a crime.[10]

A second example of English criminal law being out of step with society is to be found in the rebuttable presumption which existed until 1925 that when a married woman committed a felony other than murder or treason in the presence of her husband, she was acting under his coercion. It was this presumption which caused Mr. Bumble to declare in Charles Dickens' *Oliver Twist* 'If the law supposes that . . . the law is a ass – a idiot'. But this whole topic is best left until the next chapter.[11]

Other instances also spring to mind: the old rules on larceny by a bailee and 'breaking bulk'; the difficulties in distinguishing in individual cases between larceny by a trick and obtaining by false pretences. We need not go into these,[12] but I cannot bear to pass over in silence that, for obtaining by false pretences, the false representatations had to be about present or past facts. A lie relating to the future told with fraudulent intent or a fraudulent promise was not sufficient for the commission of the crime. Thus, in *R. v. Dent*[13] a pest destroyer who entered into contracts with farmers to destroy the moles on their land for 12 months, who received half the annual charge in advance but had no intention of carrying out the contract, was not guilty of obtaining by false pretences. Finally, as Lord Devlin pointed out in 1959, the greater part of the law relating to sexual offences was created by statute and did not correspond to the moral ideas of the majority. He wondered whether the legislature selected the offences haphazardly.[14]

I hope that by this point I have given sufficient examples for the proposition that English law, as previously Roman law, has been much out of step with society. If I have not and if it cannot be accepted that Roman law and English law have diverged from the needs and wishes of their society to a significant extent then this book has failed in its purpose. If that proposition can be accepted then it is scarcely necessary, I believe, to establish that the same was true of civil law systems before codification or of other common law systems before the days of committees established with a view to systematic law reform.

According to Oliver Wendell Holmes, 'The life of the law has not been logic; it has been experience.'[15] Despite the great insight, the sentence is not wholly accurate. I should like to suggest 'The life of the law has not been logic: it has not been experience: it has been borrowing.' In general the most important element in legal development has been the transplanting of legal rules, principles and systematics from one jurisdiction to another.[16] Nowhere is this more obvious than in what is called the 'Reception' of Roman law, and the spread of civil law systems beyond Europe into, for instance, South America. But a rule which was unsatisfactory at Rome is not too likely to fit its new domicile better. And a rule which was satisfactory even after centuries of life at Rome may be less in harmony with social conditions and values in Holland, Spain or Louisiana. Certainly one must not overlook the fact that modifications would frequently be made in the rules or their interpretation when they were transplanted and that this could lead to genuine improvements in their relationship with society. Yet, nonetheless, the extent to which borrowing is the dominant mode of development, and the minor nature of most of the modifications, mean that many rules of foreign origin cannot fit perfectly the society in which they now operate.

But in pre-codified Europe as a whole a further fact was decisive in ensuring that law and society would not be in great harmony, namely the absence of efficient legislatures which were busy with keeping private law up to scratch. The extent of the continuous and watchful role played by legislation in the development of private law naturally varied from time to time and from place to place, but a glance at any modern account of the growth of law before the intro-duction of codes provides instant verification that all in all legisla-tion was not prominent,[17] even though, it is true, there has been a tendency to underestimate it. Mediaeval legislation, itself, like other forms of law making at all times, had a tendency to survive: for England think of *Quia Emptores*, Statute of Uses, and, rather later, Statute of Frauds. It has recently been pointed out[18] that thirteenth century statutes in collections were still more or less living law in France in 1723, Venice in 1729, the Holy Roman Empire in 1747, Naples–Sicily in 1786; and that in lands only indirectly affected by the French Revolution, such laws existed even into the nineteenth and twentieth centuries; in Sardinia in 1805, Schleswig in 1819, Aragon in 1866, Castille in 1885, Hungary in 1900, Scotland in 1908, Iceland in 1932, England in 1951, Ireland in 1956, Navarre in 1966. More important is the indirect continuing life of these laws in individual institutions taken over in modern codifications.

In modernising the law and fitting it for contemporary local practice the greatest contribution in pre-codified Europe was made by jurists especially perhaps the University professors of law.[19] But however free their interpretation – and it could at times be very free[20] – they were nonetheless bound by the existing material at their disposition, and in particular by Justinian's *Corpus Juris Civilis*.

To illustrate both how difficult it is to regard law and society in pre-codified Europe as being in a proper relationship of harmony, and the skill of the academic jurists in coping with the problems, we may glance at seventeenth century Holland, and in particular at Simon van Groenewegen's *Tractatus de legibus abrogatis et inusitatis in Hollandia vicinisque regionibus* ('Treatise on the abrogated and disused laws in Holland and neighbouring regions') which was first published in Leiden in 1649. The laws in question are, of course, the Roman laws and Groenewegen is using the term 'leges' to cover any rule of Roman law, however it was first created, which was contained in Justinian's *Corpus Juris Civilis*. The very idea of writing such a book in 1648 – not on the rules of Roman law which were in use, but on the rules which had been abrogated or were not in use or had been altered – is striking evidence of the bizarrerie of legal growth. Such a book has point only if – as was indeed the case – the greater bulk of Roman law was received, and Roman law, with many of its warts plus new maladies which emerged during immigration, was fundamentally the law in force. The need for Groenewegen's work is shown in that it subsequently ran into several editions and as late as 1908 a start was made on publishing a translation into English for South Africa.[21] Indeed, more recently still, the South African Law Revision Committee requested Professor B. Beinart to translate the work, and the first and second volumes, have appeared with the dates of 1974 and 1975.[22] Nor was Groenewegen's the only or earliest work of this type. One might mention, for instance, a book which Groenewegen used, namely Philibert Bugnyon, *Traicté des loix abrogées et inusitées en toutes les Cours du royaume de France* which was first published at Lyons in 1563, and which also ran into several editions, of which one was as late as 1802. Later editions extend the scope to include other countries as well. An insight into the importance of Groenewegen's work in the present context is given by a look at the opening section of the book on the *proemium* to Justinian's *Institutes*. Groenewegen emphasises that to discover the law in force was no easy matter. First in effect one had to find out what the Roman law was on the subject. Then one had to see if the rule had been directly abrogated by statute or affected by custom or had fallen into disuse. Next one had to consider whether indirectly, by implication, a change had been made as a consequence of some other change. And in cases of doubt one had to pay attention to what was done in neighbouring regions. A modern reader is immediately struck by the extent of the confusion. Even if the final solution reached by the law was satisfactory, the time taken to find the law would be extortionate and the scope for dispute over-great, with resultant economic ill effects. The situation could scarcely be regarded as ideal. Yet the position was even more complicated than is suggested by Groenewegen. The different legal scholars also varied widely in their approaches. The difficulty was not just that on a particular practical question opinion might divide. Rather, in their published works some seventeenth century jurists took a much more academic, hence more Roman, line than others. When an uninitiated person today reads, let us say, Grotius, Vinnius, Huber, J. Voet and Noodt, he will find it difficult to determine what the law in force was. Contemporary reputation might sort this out to some extent, yet the approach of a professor could have a permanent effect on the way his ex-students saw law in practice.

To show the difficulties in finding the law in such circumstances the best approach would be to look at actual cases.[23] I have selected for discussion one from South Africa which still has an uncodified legal system deriving from Roman law since the law of the Province of Holland came to South Africa on April 7, 1652 when possession of the Cape of Good Hope was taken for the Dutch Republic. The case in question[24] was decided in 1927 – almost three centuries after Groenewegen was writing – and the basic points discussed were in effect whether, in the absence of negligence on the part of a dog's owner, he was liable to pay damages for loss which the animal caused; whether such an owner's liability could be excluded if some intervening person (not involved in the action) had been negligent; and whether the owner could limit his liability to the surrender of the offending animal. The case extends to 69 pages in the law reports, and three of the judges present discussed in some detail the Roman and Roman–Dutch authorities as well as the South African. The opinion of one judge alone, Kotzé, J. A. takes 36 pages. Innes, C. J. expressed his opinion that the facts were few and simple, but the legal position was complicated, and that it would be convenient first to examine Civil law, then the modifications to it in (a) Holland and (b) South Africa. For Roman law he starts with the *actio de pauperie*, the main action for damage caused by animals, which was in the XII Tables, a code of the mid-fifth century B.C. In discussing this he refers to the opinions of such later jurists as Glück, Pothier and von Vangerow. Then he turns to the action established by the Edict of the curule aediles which concerned the keeping of certain kinds of animals in a public place,[25] and finally to the *lex Aquilia* a statute of about 287 B.C. and which concerned damage to property. As for Holland, Innes admits that the authorities are confusing because they do not always distinguish one basis of liability from another, sometimes they rely on local Ordinances and Keuren as if they were of general application, sometimes upon the laws and customs of other Provinces. As Groenewegen emphasised right at the beginning of his book which has already been referred to, in some districts, for instance Friesland, Roman law was treated as much more authoritative than in others. Hence it was necessary for Innes in discussing the authorities to note that for example Wissenbach was a professor of law at Franeker University in Friesland, that Oosterga and Paul Voet were professors at Utrecht, that Wesembecius and Strykius were concerned with the law of Saxony. Many juristic authorities were cited from various regions and centuries: Vinnius, Busius, Wesembecius, Gortius, Groenewegen, Boehmer, Hahn, Strykius, Wissembach, Damhouder, Kersteman, Matthaeus, Oosterga, Sande, Grotius, van der Linden, Schorer, van der Keessel, Scheltinga, J. Voet, Decker, van Leeuwen, P. Voet. Innes also referred to the Criminal Ordinance of Charles V, and to Law 2.3 of the Province of Friesland. Only thereafter could he turn directly to South African law. Enough has been said, I think, to give some idea of the complexities. But Kotzé in his turn went into the matter with still greater thoroughness, citing such foreigners as Domat and Cujas, Ayliffe, even that early Germanic work the *Sachsenspiegel*, and various statutes and local ordinances.

The problem, of course, was by no means restricted to Holland in the seventeenth century and to contemporary South Africa. It existed all over Western Europe until the advent of codes. The Pandectist school in nineteenth century Germany made specially heroic efforts to homologate Roman law, legislation and custom, and to fit the result to the new industrial world. That the end product could not be regarded as perfect for German society was in the circumstances inevitable, and these academic jurists should not be blamed. Indeed, their writings can be regarded as testimony to the truth contained in Roscoe Pound's view of law as 'social engineering'. Of these Pandectists the most famous is Bernhard Windscheid who says some very illuminating things in the preface to the first edition of his *Lehrbuch des Pandektenrechts*:[26]

In addition I have tried to speak German as much as possible, in expression as well as in substance. As far as the expression is concerned, I am not of the opinion of those who see no evil or even, indeed, an advantage in the retention of Roman terminology even for contemporary law. I believe that to a real Germanification of Roman law also belongs the borrowing of the German word so far as this is possible without pedantic purism. In any event, our codes should speak German, and we ought never to forget that at all times textbooks will exercise a not unimportant, direct or indirect, influence upon the construction of these. As for the substance as well, my aim has always everywhere been directed to removing the specifically Roman appearance from the legal statements which I have brought forward, and to bring out their kernel which is still living today. On the other hand I will fear no criticism on the score that I have produced Roman legal statements, even where they seem strange to us, as living law if I was unable to produce a specific reason for their non-existence.

So long as Roman law has statutory force in Germany one must, in my opinion, hold fast to that principle if an unbearable confusion is not to arise. Certainly, than working though the received foreign law as a whole nothing is so suited to awaken and increase the wish and desire that it should at last be our lot to be freed from so many intrinsically dead legal rules in a quicker and surer way than is possible by the method of customary law. Customary law, which sees itself in the main directed along the road of practice; this, so often named and yet, so often!, undiscoverable practice!

For our purposes this admirably explicit passage from Windscheid needs no elaboration. But one may emphasise that Roman law was living law in Germany, except in so far as it had been modified by custom – interestingly Windscheid says nothing of statute – and custom was, in his view, much too slow in producing change and also difficult to discover. Specifically to avoid confusion one had, in Windscheid's opinion to hold fast to the Roman rule unless it could be shown to be no longer living law. Ironically perhaps in view of what he says about Germanifying the law, Windscheid's *Pandektenrecht* was very much used and appreciated and regarded as being of great authority in Greece where the *Hexabiblos* of about 1345 was brought into force under a decree of 1835 until a civil code could be issued. When eventually a Greek Civil Code did come into effect on February 23, 1946, it was very heavily influenced by German legal science as a result of the work of Windscheid and his Pandectist colleagues.

The introduction of a civil code of the modern type marks the beginning of a new relationship between law and society, and the subject of codes is best left until a different time though a little will be said rather later in this book. But some preliminary points should be made at this stage. Codes – and the setting up of commissions to consider the systematic reform of the law – emerge from a tendency towards rationalisation. Whether codes succeed in removing absurdities from the law and from its relation with society, or fail in whole or in part to do so is a matter of equal significance for the general view propounded in this volume. Should the latter occur then the theory argued in this book receives a strong and unnecessary confirmation. Should the former happen then we have a function of codification which should be stressed.

Notes

1. For contemporary criticism of Roman law see D. Nörr, *Rechtskritik in der römischen Antike* (Munich, Bayerische Akademie der Wissenschaften, phil. hist. Klasse, 77, 1974).
2. Treasons were distinguished from felonies by procedural rules. Some definitions also excluded summary offences from the category of misdemeanours.
3. J. F. Stephen, *History of the Criminal Law of England* 2 (London, Macmillan, 1883), p. 192.
4. *History* 2, p. 193.
5. See, e.g. Stephen, *History* 1 (1883), p. 193; accepted by R. Cross & P. A. Jones, *An Introduction to Criminal Law*, 4th edit. (London, Butterworths, 1959), p. 122, but doubted by them in their 5th edit. (1964), p. 130.
6. *Walters v. W. H. Smith & Son Ltd.* [1914] 1 K.B. 595.
7. *Christie v. Leachinsky* [1947] A.C. 573; [1947] 1 All E.R. 567.
8. *Smith v. Selwyn* [1914] 3 K.B. 98. The case has been narrowly construed. Now civil and criminal proceedings are usually concurrent.
9. See J. C. Smith & B. Hogan, *Criminal Law*, 1st edit. (London, Butterworths, 1965), pp. 72ff. For the present law see their 3rd edit. (1973), pp. 92ff.
10. For the present law see Smith & Hogan, *Criminal Law*, 3rd edit., pp. 597ff.
11. See infra, p. 93.
12. But see, e.g. Stephen, *History* 3 (1883), pp. 160ff; Smith & Hogan *Criminal Law*, 1st edit., pp. 356ff, 413ff; Cross & Jones, *Introduction* 5th edit., pp. 195ff, 232ff.
13. [1955] 2 Q.B. 590.
14. Now in Patrick Devlin, *The Enforcement of Morals* (Oxford University Press, London, 1965), p. 1.
15. *The Common Law* (Boston, Little, Brown & Co., 1881 and subsequent printings), p. 1.
16. See for the argument Watson, *Legal Transplants*, especially pp. 95ff.
17. See, e.g. F. H. Lawson, *A Common Lawyer Looks at the Civil Law* (Ann Arbor, University of Michigan Law School, 1953), especially, pp. 138ff; M. Cappelletti, J. H. Merryman, J. M. Perillo, *The Italian Legal System* (Stanford, Stanford University Press, 1967), pp. 1ff; and, above all, the detailed account by A. Wolf in H. Coing (ed.), *Handbuch der Quellen und Literatur der neuren europäischen Privatrechtsgeschichte* 1 (Munich, Beck, 1973), pp. 517ff.
18. By A. Wolf in Coing (ed.) *Handbuch*, p. 519.
19. See for France, A.-J. Arnaud, *Les Origines doctrinales du Code Civil français* (Paris, Pichon et Durand-Auzias, 1969).
20. For a few instances see Watson, *Legal Transplants*, pp. 27ff, 57ff.
21. By Vincent Sampson (Cape Town, Juta).

22. (Johannesburg, Lex-Patria Publishers).
23. For the methods used in deciding cases in eighteenth century Italy see G. Gorla, 'A Decision of the *Rota Fiorentina* of 1780 on Liability for Damages Caused by the "Ball Game" ', *Tulane Law Review* 49 (1975), pp. 346ff.
24. *O'Callaghan v. Chaplin* 1927 A.D. 310.
25. Innes seems to date this edict much earlier than I would.
26. (Düsseldorf, 1862).

Chapter 8

LEGAL SCAFFOLDING

Several times before mention has been made of the development of a back-up system, a scaffolding of legal rules which is dictated by the need to modify the rather more basic rules. This legal scaffolding is of special interest in the present enquiry and we shall examine some particular examples.

To start with an instance which has already been mentioned; from its origins probably in the third century B.C. until at least the second century A.D. the Roman consensual contract of sale did not contain an inherent warranty against eviction or against latent defects. The scaffolding which developed to cope involved remedies provided by the aedilician edict for sales in the streets and market places, and above all, the taking of a stipulation or stipulations from the seller by the buyer. But this scaffolding, as has already been argued,[1] was not satisfactory because it removed from sale one of the great advantages of a consensual contract, namely that it could be made at a distance, by letter or by messenger. Valid stipulations required oral question and answer by the parties, though the result could be satisfactory if the question was put by a son or slave of the principal contracting party.

But the scaffolding in this case had yet another defect, one which is indeed inevitable. Apart from the fact that it was inefficient and reduced the advantages of the contract of sale, the scaffolding here made the law much more complex than would otherwise have been necessary. To demonstrate this, we can limit our gaze to the stipulations against eviction. This type of stipulation, in the first instance, was for what the parties agreed, for instance for the buyer's interest when he was evicted or for double the price. A stipulation for the latter amount was normally given where what was sold was a *res mancipi* (which was not being mancipated) or a *res nec mancipi* of high value. Sale, of course, was a *bonae fidei* contract, and it came to be felt that it was in accordance with good faith for the seller to give the appropriate stipulation. Hence eventually the action on the purchase, the *actio ex empto*, could be brought against the seller to compel him to give the appropriate stipulation. Then if the buyer were evicted from the thing he could bring an action on that stipulation against the seller. The earliest textual evidence which we have shows that the stipulation for the buyer's interest could be compelled from the very early second century A.D.,[2] that for double the price from later in the same century.[3] Not long after this development, the seller was held liable on the *actio ex empto* simply as if he had given the appropriate stipulation.[4] Justinian does not seem to have made any real modification of the law here and differences could continue to exist, depending on whether the action was raised as if on a stipulation for double the price or for the buyer's interest.[5]

Moreover, so long as the buyer had to make his own protection by stipulation, drafting questions might land him into difficulties. Thus, a stipulation in what might seem the simplest form – 'Spondesne habere licere?' 'spondeo', 'Do you promise I will be permitted to retain?' 'I promise' – was regarded by at least the famous Ulpian as having limited effect. In his view, such a stipulation meant that no one was to interfere with the buyer's possession; that is, the seller was promising that everyone would allow the buyer to possess. Therefore, he says, the seller seems to have promised the acts of another, but no one can bind himself by promising the acts of another, and this is the law in force. By such a stipulation, Ulpian claims, the promisor binds himself and also his heir not to evict the promisee. Thus if the buyer was evicted from the thing by anyone else he had no remedy on the stipulation against the seller. The proper course in Ulpian's view was for the stipulation to state that a penalty or the promisee's interest was to be paid if eviction occurred.[6]

A further instance of complexity and scaffolding can again be drawn from the Roman law of scale. The ancient code of the XII Tables apparently contained a provision that when *traditio*, delivery, was made upon a sale ownership[7] was not transferred unless the price was paid or security given. This rule seems to have become unpopular and was in effect got rid of by the jurists in the late Republic or early Empire who added a third, apparently minor, qualification, 'unless the price was paid, or security given, or the seller followed the faith of the buyer'. But every time delivery was made without the seller receiving the price or security, he would be relying on the faith of the buyer, hence the rule in effect had become that on a sale *traditio* transferred ownership. But the rule of the XII Tables with the qualification which took away its effect is to be found repeated in D.18.1.19 (Pomponius *31 ad Quintum Mucium*) and J.2.1.41. What Justinian's compilers thought the law was on the subject is not in the least clear.[8] The law appears in a prima facie confusing guise; a simple proposition is made to look extremely complicated.

These two cases have in common that the innovations which improved the legal rule but made the law more complex were the result of juristic intervention with presumably the approval of those who controlled the operation of the courts. A legal change which could have reformed the law and yet kept a simple rule could only have been made by a person or body with fully recognised law-making powers, an Emperor or legislative assembly. Such person or body could, for instance, have declared 'Transfer by *traditio* on a sale transfers ownership'. Jurists could only take the provision of the XII Tables and alter its basic effect by adding a further (and perplexing) qualification. As we shall see, one of the main reasons for law being out of step with society is that law-making bodies do not intervene enough to keep the law in touch with society's needs. Modifications are made, not always surreptitiously, by judges or jurists who have much more limited powers, often indeed apparently only of law-finding and not of law-making. Inevitably such judges or jurists have to shore up the existing structure and the law becomes more complex and difficult for the ordinary person to understand.[9] When law is left to be developed by juristic interpretation or by judicial decision it is easier to make new law than to abrogate old law. Here we can, with Roscoe Pound, rightly talk of 'social engineering' by judges and jurists. But at its very best – which can happen only occasionally – it is still very much a second best. If one subscribes to the view that all law is class law then one has to say that those in charge of legalities do not feel a deep need to keep private law in line with the apparent needs of society; that this role is to a very considerable extent delegated in effect to judges or jurists who, however, are not put into a position where they can do the job efficiently or effectively.

But one other intriguing thought arises from the very first glance at legal scaffolding. The scaffolding develops and flourishes because of a divergence between law and society, when this divergence has been recognised by those with some say in shaping the law, when at least one way of improving the law has been devised. The existence of scaffolding is undesirable in absolute terms, but is welcomed or tolerated faute de mieux. Scaffolding owes its existence to a failure of the legislative body to act in these circumstances. Hence the very existence of scaffolding proves that when legislation is introduced on a particular point of private law it is not just that the law has come to be recognised as defective for the needs of society, or that society has changed and law must respond, or that the degree of legal expertise has reached the level necessary for a satisfactory reform. Something more must be involved. Historical factors will explain why any law is passed at the time it is passed; but these factors need not be deeply embedded in the life and desires of society or the technical skills of the law-makers. What holds good for a particular law may hold good (or may not) for legal reforms of a whole era. Do great periods of legal reform from the top correspond to periods of great social awareness, of social change or of heightened legal skill? An answer cannot just be assumed.

English land law provides an instructive example of scaffolding in the development of the use, which is the basis of the modern law of trusts. Even before Domesday it was common for one person to deal with land *ad opus* – *opus* gradually became *use* – i.e. on behalf of, another, when a landowner who had to be absent for a time conveyed his land to a friend *ad opus* of his wife and children. In time the device became generalised and A would transfer his land by a common law conveyance to B the *feoffee to uses* who agreed to hold it to the use of A or of C, the *cestui que use*. Prominent in this development were the Franciscans; since their order prescribed perfect poverty they could own nothing, but they did need somewhere to sleep, and land would be conveyed to the borough community to the use of the Franciscans. According to Maitland it was not before 1320 that one person was holding land generally and permanently to the use of another.

The effect of this arrangement was that the *feoffee to uses* was the common law landholder, and the *cestui que use* had no connection with the estate. Moreover, he had no common law action for redress if the *feoffee to uses* abused his position. From about 1400 the Chancellor was intervening when a *feoffee* failed to carry out directions or alienated land for his own advantage. He could not, and did not, interfere with the common law courts but he used his growing equity jurisdiction to give an action *in personam* against the *feoffee*. The *cestui que use* came to be regarded as the true owner by equity. The advantages of putting lands in use were numerous and great. Land in effect became devisable because the *feoffee* could be told how to deal with the land after the death of the beneficial owner. Conveyances could be made more easily; common law conveyances had to be open and notorious, the transfer of a use required no formalities. Settlements of land were facilitated. The feudal burdens exigible at the death of a tenant could be avoided; a number of joint *feoffees to uses* could be appointed (and replaced) and, provided the number never fell to nil, these feudal burdens never became due. The death of the *cestui que use* had no effect. Finally the use could be used to avoid forfeiture and escheat and to evade the mortmain statutes.

The use was a very popular device and by the early sixteenth century perhaps more than half of the freehold land was held in use. But to the King it represented a very great financial loss in feudal dues. Henry VIII was determined to abolish it and eventually the Statute of Uses to that effect was passed in 1536. The technique of that statute was that the use was 'executed' and the *cestui to use* became the owner of the legal estate. Though a long preamble made the Statute appear to be a popular reform the exact opposite was the truth, and it had to be forced on a very reluctant Parliament. Apart from the King, the common lawyers were the beneficiaries partly because the common law estates which resulted from the attack on uses came to be within the scope of their practice, partly because they had avoided the enquiry into common law abuses with which Henry had threatened them.

Since the Statute of Uses was so disliked – it was one cause of the Pilgrimage of Grace – it was probably inevitable that something like the *status quo ante* would eventually be restored. By steps which are much disputed by modern scholars[10] it came to be considered that the Statute did not 'execute' a second use, a use upon a use. A devise in the form 'to A and his heirs to the use of B and his heirs to the use of C and his heirs' would now mean that A still got nothing, B would get the legal estate, and C would get the equitable estate. When this happened is not clear but in the second half of the seventeenth century the Chancellor was generally enforcing second uses, and the practice was well established by 1700. The form became 'to A and his heirs to the use of B and his heirs in trust for C and his heirs' and then 'unto and to the use of B and his heirs in trust for C and his heirs'. As a result of the compromise Statute of Wills of 1540, and the abolition of military tenures in 1660 the King (and hence his Chancellor) had no real interest in obstructing the creation of uses. In any event the royal finances had been more securely organised.[11]

The story of uses will provide comfort both to adherents of the theory of social engineering and to Marxists. For us, apart from the very complexity of the scaffolding and the demonstration that scaffolding requires to be supported by further scaffolding, the main point of interest is the slow speed of development and the very low profile of the legislature. The development was left to the courts and the Chancellor. What the landowners wanted, what was in their interests – and scarcely detrimental to anyone except the King – must early have been obvious yet no statute was introduced to speed the process. Most striking of all is the absence of legislation after 1660, when the King's interest in the non-existence of uses was minimal. Again the Chancellor and the courts were left to cope with the confused mess. Apart from a short period immediately after 1536, when presumably Henry was satisfied, the law could scarcely be said to correspond to the needs or desires of society or its leaders. It is equally striking that Henry's legalisation was purely fiscal in intent. It was not Henry's aim to have a statute which best suited the people's needs or, indeed, his own on land tenure. All that Henry was interested in was restoring his finances. Exactly what the legal rules on land-holding were were irrelevant to him. He adopted the course he did simply because the use could be represented as an abuse, and his taxing aim did not have to appear too prominently.[12] The land owning classes had other legitimate interests in the existence of the use apart from the avoidance of feudal burdens, but no concern was shown for these interests. Valuable confirmation of this point of view is provided by the Statute of Wills of 1540 which allowed a tenant to devise all his socage land and two-thirds of the land he held in Knight Service. This statute was necessary because of the anger aroused when the right to leave land by will had been taken away by the Statute of Uses.[13]

It would be very easy to heap up further illustrations of scaffolding from material already covered – witness, from the English law of defamation, 'fair comment' and the 'rolled-up plea' – but this would scarcely be profitable.[14] To show that the phenomenon – in some of its daftest aspects – is not restricted to private law one example from English criminal law may suffice.

The long-lived, but now obsolete (since 1827), 'benefit of clergy' has had a deep influence in the shaping of the criminal law.[15] In the time of Bracton, a clerk of whatever order or dignity who was seized and imprisoned for the death of a man or for any other crime had to be delivered up without any inquisition if an application was made for him in the Court Christian by the ordinary.[16] In the reign of Henry VI the practice was settled that the clerk had to be convicted before he could claim this benefit of clergy. The Statute *pro clero* of 1350[17] enacted that all manner of clerks, secular as well as religious, were to be entitled to the privilege, and secular clerks were not persons in orders but their assistants in performing Divine offices, hence their 'Doorkeepers, Readers, Exorcists and Subdeacons'. The courts, perhaps not unreasonably, perhaps because they were unhappy with the severe penalty for felony, extended benefit of clergy to all who could read whether or not they were tonsured or wore clerical dress. The test of their reading ability was the first verse of the fifty-first psalm. Since this fact was known, even the illiterate male could usually avoid his fate. But women apart from nuns – and nuns only till the Reformation – could not claim clergy. Another, exception which has been described as almost grotesque[18] was that a 'bigamus' was excluded from clergy, an exception which was recognised by the statutes, 4 Edw. 1, c.5 (1276) and 18 Edw. 3, c.2 (1344). A 'bigamus' was not our bigamist, but a man who married a second wife on the death of the first, or who married a widow. The statute 4 Hen. 7, c.13 (1487) enacted that a person convicted of a clergyable offence – not all offences or all felonies were clergyable – was to be branded in his thumb with M if the charge had been murder, and T for theft, and would not be allowed to claim clergy a second time unless he actually was in orders.

On the subject Stephen is prompted to write:

> The result of this was to bring about for a great length of time a state of things which must have reduced the administration of justice to a sort of farce. Till 1487 any one who knew how to read might commit murder as often as he pleased, with no other result than that of being delivered to the ordinary to make his purgation with the chance of being delivered to him 'absque purgatione'. That this should have been the law for several centuries seems hardly credible, but there is no doubt that it was. Even after 1487 a man who could read could commit murder once with no other punishment than that of having M branded on the brawn of his left thumb, and if he was a clerk in orders he could till 1547 commit any number of murders apparently without being branded more than once.[19]

18 Eliz. c.7 ss.2, 3 (1576) abolished purgation and laid down that persons taking clergy should be discharged from custody subject only to a power in the judge to imprison them for any term not exceeding a year.[20]

But scaffolding needs support from more scaffolding. Thus, it seems that it was the fact that women were not clergyable that led to the rebuttable presumption that, if a married woman committed a crime of certain types in the presence of her husband, her husband had coerced her. Before the presumption existed, if a husband and wife together committed a clergyable felony the husband would escape hanging, the wife would not. It was abolished by the Criminal Justice Act 1925, s.47. The presumption is instructive for our understanding of legal scaffolding. First, apart from further complicating the law, it did not adequately meet the needs of the case. An unmarried woman who committed the felony or a married woman who acted in the absence of her husband could still expect to be hanged. Moreover the presumption could be rebutted. Secondly, the presumption long survived its function. 21 Jas. 1, c.6 (1622) gave women a privilege akin to that of clergy for larceny of goods worth more than 1 shilling but not more than 10 shillings; and 4 Will. and Mary, c.9 (1692) put women on the same footing as men.

Again, in 1547 the statute 1 Edw. 6, c.12 s.10 took away benefit of clergy from cases of murder. But clergy remained for manslaughter, culpable homicide without 'malice aforethought'; until 1822 (3 Geo. 4 c.84), the maximum punishment for manslaughter was burning in the hand and a year's imprisonment. It was the very mildness of the penalty here which seems to have led judges to develop the doctrines of 'constructive malice aforethought'. A person who in the course of a felony or in resisting arrest killed someone by means which were not likely to have that effect and who never intended to kill was under that doctrine guilty of murder. The unfortunate 'constructive malice aforethought' was abolished by s.1 of the Homicide Act, 1957.[21]

It might be suggested that benefit of clergy, resting as it did on the power position of the Church, is a splendid support for the Marxist view of law. And, indeed, in a sense it is. But the power situation is not a full explanation. It cannot account for the mess, for rules which benefited neither Church nor State nor represented any valuable compromise between them, nor for the survival for so long of very inappropriate law.

The scaffolding need not be created by judge or jurist. At Rome one dimension of scaffolding was in effect given official recognition. Praetors (and other magistrates) had the authority to issue edicts setting out the law they would enforce in their courts. Technically they had no power to make new law, but nothing is more obvious than that they did do so in fact. Praetorian edicts were the main method by which law developed during the later Roman Republic. In a different way in England, the Chancellor's Equity jurisdiction also created, as it were, a more official scaffolding.

What is one of the best examples of legal scaffolding, official or otherwise, is also provided by the praetors' activities at Rome. The praetors issued to the parties and judges *formulae* for the actions under their own Edict or at civil law. But should a praetor feel that the person requesting an action ought to have a remedy although no action was available by the civil law or under an edict, he could grant an ad hoc action, an *actio in factum* or *actio utilis* which might simply be based on the facts or which might incorporate a fiction, that is the judge was asked to proceed as if on particular (non-existent) facts. At first the granting of such an ad hoc remedy was an isolated episode but gradually it was recognised that praetors would grant an action in certain standard circumstances. The writers of legal books then took this into account in their books. These ad hoc actions are especially noticeable clustered around the *lex Aquilia* which dealt with damage to property. They were given as regularly and as much as a matter of course as actions under the statute itself. Indeed, since in some ways the action given under the statute was apparently thought too severe an *actio in factum* was given instead, and the interpretation of the statute in certain respects came – as a result of the scaffolding – to be absurdly narrow.[22]

Legal scaffolding may also result from legislation building on past legislation, or more commonly from subordinate legislation building on its enabling statute and subsequent subordinate legislation. C. K. Allen has thoroughly investigated the latter topic in English law,[23] and it is enough here to quote one of the most famous orders, Order no. 1216 of 1943.

The Control of Tins, Cans, Kegs, Drums and Packaging Pails (No. 5) Order, 1942 (a), as varied by the Control of Tins, Cans, Kegs, Drums and Packaging Pails (No. 6) Order, 1942 (b), the Control of Tins, Cans, Kegs, Drums and Packaging Pails (No. 7) Order, 1942 (c), the Control of Tins, Cans, Kegs, Drums and Packaging Pails (No. 8) Order, 1942 (d), and the Control of Tins, Cans, Kegs, Drums and Packaging Pails (No. 9) Order, 1942 (e), is hereby further varied in the Third Schedule thereto . . . by substituting for the reference 2A therein the reference '2A (I)' and by deleting therefrom the reference 2B.

This order shall come into force on the 25th day of August 1943, and may be cited as the 'Control of Tins, Cans, Kegs, Drums and Packaging Pails (No. 10) Order, 1943', and this Order and the Control of Tins, Cans, Kegs, Drums and Packaging Pails (Nos. 5–9) Orders, 1942, may be cited together as the 'Control of Tins, Cans, Kegs, Drums and Packaging Pails (Nos. 5–10) Orders, 1942–3'.

An explanatory note relates: 'The above Order enables tin plate to be used for tobacco and snuff tin lids other than cutter lid tobacco tins.' In South Africa, a person was convicted on a charge:

of contravening reg. 19(a) read with regs. 18(b) and 23 of the regulations made by the Minister of Lands published on February 2, 1962, in *Government Gazette* 169 under Notice R. 168, further read with *Government Notice* 1090 dated July 6, 1962, published in *Government Gazette* 285 of 1962, further read with *Provincial Notice* 37 of 1946, dated August 1, 1946, such regulations being made under sec. 10(1) of the Sea-Shore Act, 21 of 1935, as amended, and as read with reg. 424 of *Government Notice* 201 published in the *Government Gazette* of March 16, 1962.

The body of the charge conveyed that the defendant being an Asiatic male had entered a particular part of a sea-shore which had been reserved for the exclusive use of whites.[24]

At times much has been made of the technicality of legal language as a factor which makes law difficult to understand or approach by non-lawyers. I would like to suggest that the scaffolding which makes the law itself much more technical is an even more important factor in alienating people from law and lawyers.

Notes

1. Supra, pp. 14f.
2. D.19.1.11.8 (Ulpian *32 ad ed.*) (relates to Neratius).
3. D.21.2.37pr (Idem).
4. D.19.1.30.1 (Africanus *8 quaest.*); 21.2.2 (Paul *5 ad Sab.*); P.S. 2.17.2; C.8.44.6 [222 A.D.].
5. But Justinian did limit consequential damages to double the price; C.7.47.1 [531 A.D.].
6. D.45.1.38. The topic is a matter of controversy but see above all J.-Ph. Lévy, 'Les stipulations de garantie contre l'éviction dans la vente romaine', *RHD* 31 (1954), pp. 321ff; followed by Watson, *Obligations*, p. 86.
7. I.e., of *res nec mancipi*.
8. For this view of the development see Watson, *Obligations*, pp. 61ff; *Rome of the XII Tables*, pp. 145f. The recent divergent opinion of J. A. C. Thomas, 'Institutes 2.1.41 and the Passage of Property in Sale', *South African Law Journal* 90 (1973), pp. 150ff, is dealt with in the latter work.
9. Yet it should not be forgotten that the natural law jurists of the seventeenth and eighteenth centuries did in their writings simplify the law.
10. See, e.g. J. L. Barton, 'The Statute of Uses and the Trust of Freeholds', *LQR* (82) 1966, pp. 215ff, for a discussion of the cases.
11. For views on the general development of the use see *Cheshire's Modern Law of Real Property*, 11th edit. by E. H. Burn (London, Butterworths, 1972), pp. 44ff; R. E. Megarry and H. W. R. Wade, *Law of Real Property*, 3rd edit. (London, Stevens, 1966), pp. 156ff; Barton, 'Statute of Uses'; and the authorities they cite.

12. Though it was expressed in the preamble.
13. Some scholars think it was a mistaken belief that the power of devise had been taken away: e.g. R. E. Megarry, 'The Statute of Uses and the Power to Devise', *CLJ* 7 (1939–41), pp. 354ff: but see E. W. Ives, 'The genesis of the Statute of Uses', *English Historical Review* 325 (1967), pp. 673ff.
14. One could also refer to the role of fictions in English law. See, e.g. Dicey, *Law and Public Opinion*, pp. 91ff.
15. See, e.g. R. Cross & P. A. Jones, *An Introduction to Criminal Law*, 6th edit. (London, Butterworths, 1968), pp. 26f; J. Bellamy, *Crime and Public Order in England in the Later Middle Ages* (London, Routledge & Kegan Paul, 1973), pp. 151ff.
16. Ch. IX 11. 298.
17. 25 Edw. 3, st. 3.
18. J. F. Stephen, *History of the Criminal Law of England* 1 (London, Macmillan, 1883), p. 461.
19. *History* 1, pp. 463f.
20. This account of benefit of clergy is primarily endebted to Stephen, *History* 1, pp. 459ff.
21. An interesting modern survival of benefit of clergy is the *allocutus*; for this see the [Donovan] *Report of the Interdepartmental Committee on the Court of Criminal Appeal*, Cmnd. 2755 (London, H.M.S.O., 1965), pp. 17f.
22. See A. Watson, 'D.7.1.13.2 (Ulpian *18 ad Sab.*): the *lex Aquilia* and decretal actions', *IURA* 17 (1966), pp. 174ff; *Obligations*, pp. 241ff.
23. See above all his *Laws and Orders*, 3rd edit. (London, Stevens, 1965); and his *Law in the Making*, 7th edit. (Oxford, Clarendon Press, 1964), pp. 531ff.
24. *S. v. Attawari* SA 1963 (4), 610.

Chapter 9

LEGAL TRANSPLANTS

It would, I hope, be generally accepted that at most times, in most places, borrowing from a different jurisdiction has been the principal way in which law has developed.[1] This is as true today when one state in the U.S.A. will take over what has been worked out in another, or when England follows New Zealand, or Scotland, Sweden or France, as in the centuries of the Reception of Roman law and earlier.

What seems more difficult to accept, though, are the implications of legal borrowing on such a scale. If the law in one country is very largely the result of borrowing from elsewhere, then what is the innate connection between a people and their land on the one hand, and their law on the other?[2] Obviously a society will not want to borrow a rule which is largely inappropriate, and it cannot be claimed that a rule of private law will suit every legal system and every society. But it does appear that many rules of private law are equally at home (or equally not at home) in a wide variety of systems and societies. Moreover, irrespective of transplanting, very many legal rules and institutions are ancient. Frequency of borrowing and the high survival rate of legal rules together mean that 'usually legal rules are not peculiarly devised for the particular society in which they now operate'.[3]

A study of legal transplants may tell us a great deal about the nature of law. For our present, rather restricted, purpose it should be stated at once that this type of development is not necessarily incompatible with the rule adopted being the best available for the borrowing system provided always that the rule chosen is selected for sound reasons, and that it – and any modifications of it – suits its new environment.

But it seems, in fact, that the factors which determine which system is borrowed from often have nothing to do with the needs of the borrowing society. In the first place, the donor system may be chosen because of the general respect in which it is held. This has been true above all of Roman law, but also of English law and, after the French revolution and the promulgation of the Code civil, of French law. At a rather later date it has also been true of

German law, as the influence on Japan and Greece shows. The phenomenon is so noticeable that it has prompted one scholar to claim that the reception of a legal system is not a question of quality, but a question of power.

In other words, a foreign law is received not because it is regarded as the best. Much more, the receptibility of a foreign legal system is a question of power, the result of at least a spiritual and cultural power position of the received law, a position of power which again is conditioned by the fact that the law is that of a strong political power, whether that power is still real or at least there exists a living memory of it and its culture.[4]

It would not be appropriate here to examine this opinion in detail. It does, however, contain truth as well as much exaggeration. Yet at the most, the power position of Rome and France may have been a *causa sine qua non*, and not the *causa causans* of the reception of their law. No doubt the remembrance of past glory would make the reception of Roman law easier in mediaeval Italy, and the theory that the Holy Roman Empire was a continuation of ancient Rome would play a very important role in Germany, but the general high quality of Roman law, the accessibility of the legal materials in the *Corpus Juris Civilis*,[5] and the richness of the materials within a reasonable compass were the final and vital determinants. Obviously Napoleon's conquests helped to spread French law even beyond the conquered territories, but the dominant influence of French law in the nineteenth century was more powerfully due to the Code civil and the absence of plausible rivals. For us, the important fact is that once a system is regarded with enough respect, its rules will be borrowed even when the particular rule is inefficient and inappropriate.

The western world, indeed, has been so influenced by Roman law that in many situations in most countries it is impossible to see law except in Roman terms. Thus, the basic division into public and private law; the scope of the various civil codes which largely restrict their substantive law to what was contained in Justinian's Institutes; classifications such as the 'law of 'persons' – only very recently has the classification 'family law' come to be recognised; jurisprudential constructs such as possession; particular institutions such as sale and hire and the line which divides one from another. Often it is only when one looks at a very different system that one appreciates that a different approach is also possible.[6]

Thus, throughout the western world, in countries very diverse economically, socially and politically, the contract of sale is very recognisably the Roman *emptio venditio* as it was by the end of the second century A.D. Minor variations exist, of course, between one country and another, but the insidious influence of Roman law becomes apparent if one looks, for instance, at transfer of risk. At Rome, ownership of the thing sold passed to the buyer only when the thing was physically delivered to him,[7] but risk of the thing deteriorating or perishing passed to the buyer when the contract became perfect which was usually the moment of agreement.[8] This ruling may not seem logically perfect, and the French Code civil enacted that ownership and risk should pass together, namely at the moment of agreement.[9] The German Bürgerliches Gesetzbuch makes ownership and risk pass together to the buyer but only at the moment of delivery.[10] Swiss law reverted to Roman law; by the Schweizerisches Obligationenrecht[11] risk passes to the buyer when the sale is perfect; by the Schweizerisches Zivilgesetzbuch ownership is transferred only with delivery.[12] The variations owed nothing to social, economic or political conditions in these three countries, but much to the attitudes of lawyers.[13] 'In a matter so relevant to the legal profession and its work and so utterly irrelevant to society at large, this is what is bound to happen', says Otto Kahn-Freund.[14] But the fascinating thing is that the lawyers all – explicitly or not – considered the question in terms of Roman law and minor deviations from it. The example of Rome obscured from them the possibility of a more radical solution. No system has declared that risk of destruction or deterioration before delivery should fall equally on the buyer and seller,[15] yet this seems at least as equitable as any of the solutions adopted and would be easy to operate. Again, is it fully reasonable not even to consider whether, with regard to the transfer of risk, one rule might operate where the purchaser is a housewife buying for the home, another where the purchaser is a business buying large quantities in the way of trade?[16] Or, considering that businesses trading together will make their own contract terms and even then will hesitate to involve legal rights against one another,[17] might it not be appropriate to frame the rule on transfer of risk with a particular group of sellers and purchasers, such as shopkeepers and housewives, in mind?

An instructive example on transfer of risk may also be drawn from the South African case, *Pahad v. Director of Food Supplies and Distribution*,[18] which did not actually concern a contract of sale but a form of compulsory purchase under War Measure 55 of 1946. After the time when rice belonging to the appellant was 'frozen' but before it was collected by the respondent it was stolen from the appellant's premises. Among the issues raised was the question whether risk had passed to the Director of Food Supplies and Distribution. Van den Heever, J. A. clearly regarded the rule that risk transferred to the buyer when the contract became perfect (although the thing was not delivered) both as settled South African law and as arbitrary. He continued;

As may be expected such a doctrine was unknown to the classical Roman law except in the sale of commodities such as wine which are liable to suffer autogenous deterioration, for example by fermentation or chemical reaction. In these exceptional cases the risk passed not at the conclusion of the sale but after the lapse of an arbitrarily fixed period. (Hymans, *Romeinsch Verbintenissenrecht*, 2nd ed., p. 37 *et seq.*) Where the thing sold perished before delivery, the seller was released from his obligation to deliver and the purchaser was not obliged to pay the purchase price – in other words the sale fell through. Where the codifiers have omitted to interpolate, the original rule is still apparent. (Cf. *Dig.* 18.6.13.14.15 especially L.15.1 which reads: 'Where building material is stolen after delivery, the risk is the buyer's; if before delivery the risk is the seller's – but beams marked by the buyer are deemed to have been delivered.' See too Mitteis-Levy-Rabel, *Index Interpolationum* ad LL. Cit.) The rule *periculum emptoris est* is due to wholesale interpolation by the Byzantines (Hymans, Op. & Loc. cit.). The reason is obvious. The inhabitants of the Eastern Empire could not grasp that according to Roman law ownership was transferred by delivery, a fact which emerges from a number of petitions directed to the Emperor which to a Roman would have appeared childish (*cf. Code*, 3.32.12; 4.49.6; 4.38.9.12). The Greek did not have the Roman's absolute concept of *dominium*; 'it would appear that one can only speak of stronger or weaker rights to a thing' (Pringsheim, *Der Kauf mit fremdem Geld*, p. 2). In the light of a basic concept so different from that of the Roman it is easy to understand how different conclusions may have been drawn as to the incidence of fortuitous loss in contractual relations. We have received the Roman law as corrupted by the Byzantines but that does not justify the extension by analogy of a rule which owes its origin to an accident of history, which operates in an arbitrary fashion and cannot be justified on equitable grounds, to a field of law to which it has not yet authoritatively been made to apply.[19]

The quotation is equally instructive in the present context whether one begins with the proposition that it seems to be Van den Heever's opinion that a bad rule was adopted because it was thought to be

Roman law: or that, in his opinion the bad rule need not be extended by analogy because in fact it is not Roman classical law but Justinian's Byzantine corruption. It should be remembered that Roman law is not a direct, binding source of law in South Africa: indeed, if it were, what would be binding would be the law of Justinian.[20] More illuminating still, it is very doubtful whether the rule was the result of Byzantine interpolation. It is almost universally accepted today that the rule is classical Roman law,[21] and this was also the general opinion of scholars in 1949. Yet, in opposing the spread of the rule by analogy, Van den Heever seems to have thought it desirable both to claim that the rule was interpolated and that this was recognised by scholars.[22] One can but admire the importance attached in practice to getting the Roman rule.

In the second place national pride may determine that borrowings should be made, or should be restricted, from some particular system. The consequence is not that the spiritual nationalists will then invent *de novo* but borrow from some other system. In an article published in 1956 T. B. Smith then a Professor of Scots Law and now a Scottish Law Commissioner wrote:

A modern work in English on the Roman law which had 'accommodated itself to practical needs' is urgently needed wherever both Civil Law and Common Law have been received into the same legal system. The Common Law cuckoo has already laid too many eggs in the eagle's nest.[23]

Perhaps even more emotively, in 1958, lamenting the acceptance of rules of English law the same author declared:[24]

But, alas, ... we in Scotland have gone a-whoring after some very strange gods.

A statement made to me by a Scottish Law Commissioner (with authority to publish) in early 1971 said:

... account has necessarily to be taken of English solutions even if these are eventually rejected as unsuitable for reception into Scots law. Indeed in many contexts English solutions have to be studied to identify fundamental differences from Scots law cloaked by superficial similarity. Endeavours to achieve unified solutions in the field of Contract law have in particular revealed that what has been assumed to be common ground was approached by members of the Scottish and English Contracts Teams through conceptually opposed habits of thought. Whereas English comparative research relied particularly on American and Commonwealth sources, the background of some of the Scottish proposals derived from French, Greek, Italian and Netherlands sources – and from the Ethiopian Civil Code, which was, of course, drafted by a distinguished French comparative lawyer.[25]

The Commissioners' *Seventh Annual Report 1971–72*[26] related:

We view with disfavour ill-considered attempts to unify the laws of England and Scotland by the application of principles which are not consistent with Scots law.

The Scottish Law Commission's reluctance now to engage in joint exercises with the English Law Commission is well known. Again, on a separate matter, a report in *The Scotsman* newspaper for August 16, 1974 that the Council of the Law Society of Scotland (i.e. the professional body of the solicitors) had said that steps towards the assimilation of the law and legal systems of Scotland and England are 'inevitable and desirable' and that there might be a common code led to letters of protest from academic lawyers. One paragraph from that of Professor A. B. Wilkinson[27] is particularly relevant:

It is indeed surprising after several decades marked by an increased consciousness in legal thinking of the distinctive character of Scots law and of the importance of maintaining its integrity as a separate system, that any responsible body of Scottish lawyers should see as a desirable goal the assimilation of Scots law to a system which, whatever its merits, is as substantially and, in some respects, radically distinct as in English law.

Scots law is a 'mixed system' with roots deep in the Civil Law and the Common Law. At times in her history Scotland has drawn more from one root than the other. The fascinating thing which is revealed by some of the above quotations is the very real feeling that it is better to borrow consciously from Civil Law systems (in cluding Greece and Ethiopia) than from the Common Law (in cluding England) because the former, but not the latter, is in con formity with Scottish legal principles and tradition.

If anything can be said in favour of general assimilation with the law of England, it can be said with many times greater force in favour of tracing our way back into the continental legal tradition of which we were once a part, and whose concepts and methodology are still remarkably among the most fertile and useful elements of our own jurisprudence.[28]

It cannot be too greatly emphasised that at no time has Scotland been a part of a continental legal tradition from which English law was excluded.

In a reply to the letters from which we have quoted, the Secretary of the Law Society of Scotland, R. B. Laurie, wrote:[29]

> More clearly than your correspondents, however, the council recognise that law and legal arrangements exist for the benefit of the community and not vice versa. Law is for people. They considered, for example, the needs of the business community and wrote as follows: '. . . a large measure of integration already exists in the sphere of commercial and fiscal law. Business interests in Scotland are believed to be, in general, strongly in favour of assimilation. Whether Scottish lawyers like it or not, an increasing number of businesses operating in Scotland are controlled from England (not to mention the U.S.A.) and the general view in business circles is that the question of whether Scottish or English law prevails is of less importance than that there should be one law operating throughout the whole United Kingdom.' . . . The council has taken the view (which I think would be shared by most people with social involvement, most legal practitioners, and certainly the man in the street) that, even if one has misgivings about the English measure, it is really intolerable that there should be a radical difference in the law of divorce on the two sides of the Border. This may not be a problem for your academic correspondents but it does worry practitioners who have to justify the law to their clients.[30]

Similarly in contemporary South Africa there is a bias against borrowing from English law – which has been an important source in the past – even though there may be disagreement as to when the bias first became apparent or how powerful it is. At the same time the old Roman–Dutch writings of the seventeenth and eighteenth centuries have been given greater attention.[31] One might also mention the battle in Germany before the enactment of the *Bürgerliches Gesetzbuch* between the Romanists (such as Windscheid) and the Germanists (such as Gierke) on the influence of Roman law.

A third factor which influences the choice of foreign law to be adopted, and which is independent of the quality of the law is language and accessibility.[32] The Reception of Roman law was greatly helped by the fact that the *Corpus Juris Civilis* was in Latin, a language then known to all learned men, and contained the law within reasonable dimensions. Likewise the victory of Common law over Civil Law in the United States owed much to Blackstone's

Commentaries on the Laws of England largely because they were written in English and contained so much legal detail in one work.[33] Again, the State of Louisiana and the Province of Quebec both have a Civil Law background and both have a Civil Code based primarily on French Law.[34] No one would deny that Quebec has very much a Civil Law system (though with a Common Law admixture), but the contrary has often been maintained in the case of Louisiana. At the very least, Anglo-American Common Law has been very much more influential in Louisiana than in Quebec. Why? At least part of the explanation is that the language of Quebec has remained French, that of Louisiana has become English. French sources have remained open to the former, have become closed to the latter.[35]

As a fourth factor one may mention past history. It is enough here to remark that neighbouring countries in Africa may have basically a Common Law or a Civil Law system, depending on who was the colonising power.

The converse to all of the foregoing should also be stressed. It is not the case that when it is generally known that a better rule exists elsewhere, that rule will be adopted. Let me give two examples, one ancient, one modern. Roman law underwent changes in Egypt, once Egypt had become part of the Roman Empire in 27 B.C. Thus the Romans in Egypt recognised the principle of direct agency (as had the Egyptians earlier), but this was never taken over into Roman law itself, though few would dispute the value of such a doctrine, and the metropolitan Roman jurists must have been well-aware of the principle.[36] For modern times we may take an example of importance to us all, though it is not really a matter of private law. It often happens that an innocent person is injured so severely by a car that the driver who was at fault could never pay the value of the injuries. To take care of such risks the driver is insured. In the United Kingdom automobile insurance for injury to third parties is compulsory for all drivers. Alas, from time to time it happens that a person is injured by an uninsured driver. He has no claim against anyone but the driver who frequently cannot meet the claim. Even worse, in some States in the U.S.A. insurance against third party injuries is not compulsory; even where it is, drivers will not be insured for an unlimited sum, but up to an agreed-on amount which may easily turn out to be unsatisfactory for both driver and victim. Yet the Saskatchewan Automobile Accident Insurance Act of 1946 (Chapter 11 of 1946) ensured a minimum compensation for bodily injuries or death by motor vehicle accidents on Saskatchewan highways, and the benefits were extended to Saskatchewan residents who were injured in motor vehicle accidents elsewhere in

North America (excluding Mexico). There are also subsequent improvements.[37] But clearly since then it has been obvious that any Government anywhere, at no real cost to itself since it could recoup from a levy on motorists, could introduce a system of reasonable protection for the victim (or, if one prefers, at least for innocent victims) of automobile accidents.[38]

To this point I have been arguing in this chapter that very frequently legal rules do not develop directly from the particular circumstances of the state in question which relate to the rules but are borrowed from elsewhere, and that often factors other than the high quality of the legal rules themselves or their precise fitness for the borrowing state decide the choice.

An examination of transplants throws into high relief a further factor of great importance for legal development, namely that the reasons which favour the creation and acceptance of a legal rule in more than one system need not be the same in all the systems. Very different social, political and economic circumstances may nonetheless be conducive to the creation of the same legal rule. Though this emerges most clearly from cases of legal borrowing, it can also be found in instances of independent development. One example may serve for all, and we need not here trace all its ramifications. Thus, consider the treatment of the property of a married couple. The property may remain separate to each spouse, or become the husband's or be subject to a community régime. Community property, which was unknown to Roman law, may be regulated in various ways. In one way, known as the *communauté réduite aux acquêts*, each spouse keeps what he or she had at the time of marriage (and is also responsible for debts outstanding at the time) but whatever thereafter is earned (including the revenue from property) or saved by either or both becomes common property. The share in the gains may be equal, or the wife may receive a smaller fraction, or it may be in proportion to their assets at the time of the marriage. This form of community property is to be found in a number of systems. Let us begin, unhistorically, with Northern Europe in the later Middle Ages.

For the community property system in general Otto Kahn-Freund distinguishes three main motivations which frequently overlap.[39] The first, he says, was to protect the wife who was assumed incapable of defending her own affairs; the second was to protect the survivor against the next-of-kin of the predeceasing spouse; and the third was to provide capital for the husband's enterprise. For the period from the later Middle Ages onward, Kahn-Freund stresses this third motivation.[40] Thus,

And if you go across the Channel you see how, for example, in Germany community systems began to develop among the burgesses, the merchants, the artisans of the growing towns of the late Middle Ages, and how the origin of most of our modern European and American community regimes is to be found in the great commercial centres of the Low Countries and of Northern France.

Jean Brissaud, discussing the rise of community property in France during the same period observes that community is the matrimonial system of merchants because in towns where family possessions are few, there is nothing to prove an obstacle to a community régime. The marriage portion of a wife, he tells us, consists in making an investment. In the country, community was the system of serfs and commoners, i.e. the people who held only movables.[41] Community was much less common among the land-owning nobility, a fact which, we are told, was also true in Germany.[42] Whatever the origins and earlier history of community property[43] there seems to be general agreement that in France, Germany and the Low Countries, its success lay primarily in the need for rapid capital accumulation in commercial enterprises in a society which as yet knew nothing about corporation finance – the wife's money was to work in the husband's enterprise.[44]

The particular form of community property which concerns us, the *communauté réduite aux acquêts* (which would provide against the dispersal of accumulated revenues which therefore could form capital[45]) was successful with the others. Huebner[46] estimates that by 1900 this community system operated among a population of about 10 millions in Germany, particularly as a result of legislation from 1571 to 1755, especially in the regions of the Franconian law, in parts of Hesse-Darmstadt and Electoral Hesse, in Nassau, Wetzlar, and Frankfort, in parts of the Rhine province of Prussia, Schleswig-Holstein, Hanover, Thuringia, great areas of Old Bavaria, and in Württemberg.

This form of community does seem to have had an earlier history in Germany during the period of the Franks, for instance under the Salic and Ripuarian systems and among the Westphalians.[47] How far back it actually goes and whether the system operated even during the period of the early German migrations may here be left open. But what I would like to discuss is the earliest clear literary evidence for it,[48] not in Germany but in Spain among the Visigoths. A law of King Reccesvind (who reigned between 649 and 672), which appears in the Fuero Juzgo[49] of 693, provides that where persons of equal rank marry they would share in common any gain or loss to their property in proportion to the amount each holds. Gifts after marriage, whether to the husband or the wife, were to remain the separate property of the donee who had absolute power of disposal. This law had a very successful subsequent history, but it must be admitted that we do not know whether the régime was a complete invention of Reccesvind and his advisors, or was a restatement of an existing practice. Whether it originated with Reccesvind or before, its acceptance can scarcely be explained by a need for rapid capital accumulation for the commercial enterprises of the husband. Unfortunately we do not have direct evidence for the rationale of the régime, but it has been sought, probably reasonably enough, in economic conditions. Thus de Funiak[50] argues that the reason is to be found in the wife's sharing with her husband in a hard and dangerous existence, in his daily life and labour. She, we are told, lingered on the edge of battlefields to succour him, to help him despoil his enemies, she was side by side with him in dangerous migrations, and took equal part in his councils. The same author also stresses the democratic nature of that society.

By steps which we need not consider this Visigothic form of community became established throughout Spain, though the gains were shared equally between the spouses no matter what their original financial position was at the time of marriage. From Spain this community régime was taken to the Spanish territories in the New World, including California. After the war with Mexico, California became part of the United States in 1848 by the Treaty of Guadalupe Hidalgo. A constitutional convention was held in 1849 to draft a constitution for California and one of the clauses proposed and accepted for the constitution was:[51]

All property, both real and personal, of the wife, owned or claimed by her before marriage, and that acquired afterward by gift, devise, or descent, shall be her separate property, and laws shall be passed more clearly defining the rights of the wife in relation as well to her separate property as to that held in common with the husband. Laws shall also be passed providing for the registration of the wife's separate property.

The provision itself and the debate in the Constitutional Convention[52] show that the intention was to retain the Spanish system of community which existed before California became part of the United States.[53] So strong was this desire that the provision was inserted into the Constitution not just left to subsequent legislation, hence could not simply be changed by the Legislature but only by going to the people. In accordance with the provision the first legislature enacted legislation in 1850 making clear the difference between community property and separate property and continuing the law of community which had existed previously.[54]

But what were the arguments produced in the debate in favour of community property? What comes through most is the ethical feeling that women should be well treated, whether this was expressed – strangely in view of the descent of the régime from the Visigoths – by

> The time was, sir, when woman was considered an inferior being; but as knowledge has become more generally diffused, as the world has become more enlightened, as the influence of free and liberal principles has extended among the nations of the earth, the rights of woman have become generally recognised.[55]

or

> I trust, in consideration of the peculiar necessity which must exist here for such a provision, owing to the inducements for wild and hazardous speculations, and the probability of frequent and sudden losses which would otherwise involve families in ruin; in consideration, also, of the native population of California, who have always lived under this system, that it will become a part of our fundamental law.[56]

This second quotation also reveals two other reasons; that many in California had previously lived under that matrimonial régime,[57] and that local circumstances were such that speculation was and was expected to be peculiarly common and dangerous. Thus, the emphasis – far from being on enabling the husband to accumulate capital for his business – was on preventing him using his wife's capital. Another motivation expressed was the desire for a simple system, not the confusion of the common law.[58] Finally,

> I am not wedded either to the common law or the civil law, nor as yet, to a woman; but having some hopes that sometime or another I may be wedded, and wishing to avoid the fate of my friend from San Francisco (Mr. Lippitt) I shall advocate this section in the Constitution, and I would call upon all the bachelors in this Convention to vote for it. I do not think we can offer a greater inducement for women of fortune to come to California. It is the very best provision to get us wives that we can introduce into the Constitution.[59]

Various factors, indeed, weighed more or less heavily with the different members of the Convention. Within one jurisdiction a multiplicity of reasons might favour the acceptance of a particular legal rule. (One fact which is revealing is that in the present context the members of the Convention debated only the relative merits of the common law rules and the *communauté réduite aux acquêts*. Advantages of other community systems seem to have passed unnoticed.)

Thus, societies so disparate in political, social and economic terms as, for instance, Visigothic Spain, parts of post-mediaeval Germany and nineteenth century California could accept for a variety of reasons what is basically the same régime of matrimonial property.[60] It might be claimed that these societies had in common an attitude towards women and the family which overrode more distant considerations, yet one would then wonder if this attitude in the relevant parts of Germany differed from that in other parts of Germany where a different régime prevailed, and whether the attitude to women was different in California from that in States which adopted common law rules.[61]

To illustrate the notion that a similar legal result might ensue from different factors one might choose a still wider example. Thus,

Moreover – and Max Weber's sociological analysis has made this convincingly clear – the thought processes of the common law can and should be understood as the outcome of the needs and habits of a legal profession organised in gilds and preserving the structure and power of a medieval vocational body. The modern continental systems were developed in the universities by legal scholars for the use of officials. English law evolved as a series of gild rules for the use and guidance of the members and apprentices of the Inns of Court.[62]

The idea seems plausible and the contrast between the thought processes of English lawyers and their continental counterparts appears convincing. And yet, one of the commonplaces of modern jurists – it occurs again and again – is the extreme similarity of the thought processes of the classical Roman jurists and of English lawyers.[63] Whatever the explanation of the Roman jurists' habits of thought – and we need not go into that – it cannot be the result of a 'legal profession organised in gilds and preserving the structure and power of a medieval vocational body'. Once again we have the phenomenon that different circumstances may lead to a very similar result. Particular legal rules and habits of thought are not tied to one and only one consonant social, economic, political environment.[64]

In the latter part of this chapter I have not been directly concerned with my main theme, that much of law does not accord with the needs and desires of the society in which it operates. Rather I have been pecking at the notion that a precise legal rule can only arise and continue when very particular circumstances are present. The connection of a legal rule with any one environment is less intimate than may be supposed. It is a characteristic of a legal rule to be made for and to fit into very different circumstances, both in several states and also within one state.[65]

Notes

1. There are, of course, exceptions. Roman law seems to have been relatively immune from transplants.
2. See, for instance, Watson, *Legal Transplants*; O. Kahn-Freund, 'On Uses and Misuses of Comparative Law', *MLR* 37 (1974), pp. 1ff; A. Watson, 'Legal Transplants and Law Reform', *LQR* 92 (1976), pp. 79ff.
3. Watson, *Legal Transplants*, p. 96.
4. P. Koschaker, *Europa und das römische Recht* (Munich, Biederstein, 1947), pp. 137f.
5. In general the Digest texts give only the facts relevant to the legal ruling; and they relate the jurist's opinion on the state of the law, not the verdict given in a particular case. Roman law is here in marked contrast to, say, mediaeval English law. Not only was it difficult to find the relevant cases – and it still is for historians – but the reports could include much totally irrelevant information, and the verdict might be influenced by facts other than the state of the law.
6. See Watson, *Legal Transplants*, pp. 36ff, 90ff.
7. G.2.19; D.41.1.9.3, 4, 5 (Gaius *2 rer. cott.*).
8. D.18.1.35.4 (Gaius *10 ad ed. prov.*); 18.6.8 (Paul *33 ad ed.*); 19.1.31pr (Neratius *3 membr.*).
9. Art. 1138, 1583–7; 1624.
10. §§446, 929.
11. §185.
12. §714; see also §922.
13. See Watson, *Legal Transplants*, pp. 82ff.
14. In his review of Watson's *Legal Transplants* in *LQR* 91 (1975), pp. 292ff at p. 293.
15. See D. Daube, 'The Scales of Justice', *Juridical Review* 68 (1951), pp. 109ff at p. 110.
16. There would admittedly be difficulties – not insuperable – in drawing the dividing line between each class.
17. See S. Macaulay, 'Non-Contractual Relations in Business; a Preliminary Study', *American Sociological Review* 28 (1963), pp. 55ff.

18. *SA* 1949 (3), 695.
19. P.710.
20. In another case of the same year Van den Heever, J. A. expressly accepted the view that the Court administers Roman–Dutch law and not the Roman law of Justinian: *Tjollo Ateljies (Eins.) Bpk v. Small* SA 1949 (1), 856 at 865. See also H. R. Hahlo & E. Kahn, *The South African Legal System and its Background* (Cape Town, Juta, 1968), p. 581; P. van Warmelo, 'Roman Law and the Old Authorities on Roman–Dutch Law', *Acta Juridica* (1961), pp. 38ff.
21. See, e.g. V. Arangio-Ruiz, *Istituzioni di diritto romano*, 14th edit. (Naples, Jovene, 1960), p. 342; Kaser, *RPR* 1, p. 552, and the works they cite.
22. Ironically Van den Heever would have been on very strong ground for the case in hand with a rather different argument. Although the risk is not on a seller in possession he is liable, it is generally thought (see Kaser, *loc. cit.*), for *custodia*. Hence the loss falls on him if the thing is stolen.
23. 'The Common Law Cuckoo', *Butterworths South African Law Review* (1956), pp. 147ff; reprinted in *Studies Critical and Comparative* (Edinburgh, Green, 1962), pp. 89ff.
24. 'Strange Gods' (University of Edinburgh, Inaugural Lecture no. 4, 1958), p. 1; reprinted in *Studies Critical and Comparative*, pp. 72ff.
25. Already quoted in *Legal Transplants*, p. 96. Similar phraseology is to be found earlier: 'Superficial similarities too often conceal fundamental differences which may be apparent only to those thoroughly familiar with both systems'; T. B. Smith, *Studies Critical and Comparative*, p. 96. In the case of contract it would, I believe, be more correct to say that superficial differences conceal fundamental similarities.
26. (Edinburgh, 1973, Scot. Law Com. n. 28) §12. For difficulties in reconciling differences of approach where the desired ends were agreed on see L. C. B. Gower, 'Reflections on Law Reform', *University of Toronto Law Journal* 23 (1973), pp. 257ff at pp. 264ff. See also Farrar, *Law Reform*, pp. 38ff.
27. *The Scotsman*, 21 August 1974.
28. R. Sutherland, Letter in *The Scotsman*, 21 August 1974.
29. Letter in *The Scotsman*, 24 August 1974.
30. For the expression of a rather similar view see already Watson, *loc. cit.* A reply to Laurie by Wilkinson is in *The Scotsman*, 27 August 1974. Lord Hunter, Chairman of the Scottish Law Commission added to the debate and declared 'that in certain quarters the word "assimilation" is sometimes used and understood in the sense of Scots law and the Scottish legal system being absorbed into the English system': letter in *The Scotsman*, 27 August 1975. The last letter in the series, published on 2 September 1975, was by a number of practising solicitors who supported the position of the academics.

31. See, e.g. T. W. Price, 'The Future of Roman–Dutch Law in South Africa', *SALJ* 64 (1947), pp. 494ff at p. 498; N. J. van der Merwe in his review of McKerron, *The Law of Delict, Tydskrif vir Hedendaagse Romeins–Hollandse Reg* 28 (1965), pp. 160ff at p. 165; P. Q. R. Boberg, 'Oak Tree or Acorn? – Conflicting Approaches to our Law of Delict', *SALJ* 83 (1966), pp. 150ff at p. 153; C. J. R. Dugard in his review of Smith & Hogan, *Criminal Law, SALJ* 83 (1966), pp. 234ff at p. 234; D. F. Mostert, *Die Romeins–Hollandse Reg in Oënskou* (Pretoria, Universiteit van Pretoria, 1969), p. 6; Hahlo & Kahn, *South African Legal System*, pp. 578ff.

32. See, e.g. Watson, *Legal Transplants*, pp. 93f.

33. See above all J. S. Waterman, 'Thomas Jefferson and Blackstone's Commentaries', in *Essays in the History of Early American Law*, by D. H. Flaherty (Chapel Hill, University of North Carolina Press, 1969), pp. 451ff.

34. For at least one other scholar Spanish law was the main basis of the Louisiana 'Digest' of 1808: this does not affect the present issue; for references see Watson, *Legal Transplants*, pp. 103f.

35. See, e.g. J. L. Baudouin, 'The Impact of the Common Law on the Civilian Systems of Louisiana and Quebec', in *The Role of Judicial Decisions and Doctrine in Civil Law and in Mixed Jurisdictions*, edit. by J. Dainow (Baton Rouge, Louisiana State University Press, 1974), pp. 1ff.

36. See Watson, *Legal Transplants*, p. 33.

37. See, e.g. J. Green, 'Automobile Accident Insurance Legislation in the Province of Saskatchewan', *Journal of Comparative Legislation and International Law* 31 (1949), pp. 39ff.

38. The question whether or not a negligent driver should be made liable to make compensation is disputed and is disputable. But it is a separate issue from the financial protection of the injured person and may here be set aside.

39. *Matrimonial Property: Where do we go from here?* (University of Birmingham, Josef Unger Memorial Lecture delivered 29 January 1971), pp. 25ff.

40. *Matrimonial Property*, p. 29.

41. *History of French Private Law* translated by R. Howell (London, Murray, 1912), p. 819.

42. See, e.g. R. Huebner, *History of Germanic Private Law* translated by F. S. Philbrick (London, Murray, 1918), pp. 621ff, especially at pp. 631, 645ff.

43. See also F. Pollock and F. W. Maitland, *History of English Law* 2, 2nd edit. (Cambridge, Cambridge University Press, 1968), pp. 399ff.

44. In general see Kahn-Freund, *Matrimonial Property*, pp. 28ff and the reference he gives.

45. See Kahn-Freund, *Matrimonial Property*, p. 28.

46. *Germanic Private Law*, p. 653.

47. See, e.g. Huebner, *Germanic Private Law*, pp. 627f.
48. But what must have been a not too dissimilar system appears in the Laws of Gortyn (of the mid-fifth century B.C. at the latest); Col. II. 45ff; III, 18f, 25, 32ff, 42f; VI. 9ff, 31ff; XI. 42ff; See R. F. Willetts, *The Law Code of Gortyn* (Berlin, de Gruyter, 1967), pp. 20ff.
49. 4.2.16 or 17.
50. W. Q. de Funiak, *Principles of Community Property* 1, 1st edit. (Chicago, Callaghan, 1943), pp. 27f; 2nd edit. by de Funiak & M. J. Vaughn (Tucson, University of Arizona Press, 1971), pp. 19f. In volume 2 (which has not been re-edited or republished) the author conveniently presents the most important sources.
51. Art. 11 s. 14.
52. For the debate see J. R. Browne, *Debates in the Convention of California on the Formation of State Constitution of 1849* (Washington, Towers), pp. 257ff.
53. See de Funiak, *Community Property* 1, p. 109.
54. *California Statutes* 1850, chap. 95, p. 254.
55. Mr. Dimmick in Browne, *Debates*, p. 263; see also remarks by Mr. Jones at p. 264.
56. Mr. Tefft at p. 259; see also p. 258 and Mr. Jones at p. 265, Mr. Norton at pp. 266f. Another provision of the Constitution which is intended to avoid total ruin of a family is Art. XI, sec. 15.
57. See also Mr. Dimmick at p. 263.
58. Mr. Jones at p. 264.
59. Mr. Halleck at p. 259.
60. See also the basic argument in A. Watson, 'Legal Transplants and Law Reform', *LQR* 92 (1976), pp. 79ff.
61. For similar examples on restraints on testation and on *laesio enormis* in sale see F. H. Lawson, 'Some Paradoxes of Legal History', *AJCL* 15 (1967), pp. 101ff.
62. O. Kahn-Freund in his introduction to K. Renner, *The Institutions of Private Law and their Social Functions* (London, Routledge & Kegan Paul, 1949), p. 13. Since I have used two quotations from Kahn-Freund as pegs on which to hang this part of the discussion I should like to stress that he has never claimed that a legal institution could not serve different social purposes in different social environments.
63. See, e.g., F. Pringsheim, 'The inner Relationship between English and Roman Law', now in *Gesammelte Abhandlungen* 1 (Heidelberg, Winter, 1961), pp. 76ff; W. W. Buckland and A. D. McNair, *Roman Law and Common Law*, 2nd edit. by F. H. Lawson (Cambridge, Cambridge University Press, 1952), pp. xiiiff.
64. This is also one of the lessons of Karl Renner's insight that the social function of legal rules change without a change in the rules: *The Institutions of Private Law*.
65. See too E. Rabel, 'The Statute of Frauds and Comparative Legal History', *LQR* 63 (1947), pp. 174ff.

Chapter 10

CAUSES OF DIVERGENCE

It will have already become apparent from the preceding chapters –
if it was not apparent before – that for radical law reform something
like legislation is usually needed. (For Rome I am here including
within the term 'legislation', magistrates' Edicts which were so
important in the Republic and Imperial constitutions.) It will also
have become apparent that often legislation is not forthcoming, at
least for centuries. The basic reason for this is quite simply that the
body or individual which has control over legislation on private law
often has insufficient time or interest for law reform since it is usually
charged with other functions especially of a political nature. This
would apply to the Roman magistrates, the *concilium plebis*, the
senate and the Emperors, as well as to the English King (in earlier
days) and now to the Sovereign in Parliament, and to European
legislative bodies. Indeed, the members of any legislature frequently
have no particular legal qualifications or expertise. And often their
interest in most aspects of private law is very limited. It is very
illuminating that when the revised draft of what became the German
Bürgerliches Gesetzbuch was laid before the Reichstag in June,
1896, fully one-third of the 125 speeches on it concerned rights and
liabilities relating to game and domestic animals.[1] All in all, only
one important change was made in the draft, that which reduced
from twenty-five years to twenty-one the age up to which parental
consent was need for marriage.

Circumstances are, of course, not always everywhere the same. A
strong Emperor or King such as Augustus or Louis XIV who in
general did not have to spend too much time on public debate, and
who was interested in private law, could very quickly – at little cost
in time to his other duties – make a legal reform which was obviously needed.

Other factors, too, often make legislation haphazard.

To begin with, the very fact that persons or bodies in charge of
legislation very often have a political function will diminish their
role in reforming private law. If by pressing for a reform which is
generally recognised as desirable, they could alienate even a small
number of their supporters, they may prefer to stay aloof. Thus,

for Rome between 200 B.C. and the end of the Republic – the most
fertile period of legal development the world has known – there was
no legal innovation in the relationship between a *paterfamilias*
and his dependants, no change by statute or edict on marriage or
divorce. Yet immediately thereafter Augustus was responsible for
extensive reforms. Republican politicians, concerned for their
future, stayed away from reform in a sensitive area. Augustus had
no need to.[2] In contemporary Britain the Government has been very
reluctant to involve itself in the reform of the law of divorce even
when it could be shown that only a minority opposed a change in the
law. The Divorce Reform Act 1969 (chapter 55) had to be by a
private member's bill.[3]

Again, as we have already seen, legislation drastically affecting
the development of private law may be introduced for reasons, even
the most personal reasons, affecting the ruling élite at that time,
without any concern being shown for the state of the law in general
or for other interests. Thus, the decree of the Roman senate permitting marriage with a brother's daughter was the work of senators
who wished to please the Emperor Claudius. They had no concern
with the general question of marriage reform, and if Agrippina had
been Claudius' sister's daughter, the decree would certainly have
permitted marriage with that kind of niece and retained as invalid
marriage with a brother's daughter.[4] Again, Henry VIII's Statute of
Uses was passed to increase his revenues with no concern either for
the general development of land law or for the legitimate interests of
landholders which might have been preserved while the King was in-
creasing his revenues.[5] The same may be said of Constantine's
statute of A.D. 337 on sale, probably but not certainly only of land.
The main purpose of this was to ensure that taxes on land were paid,
and the Emperor was indifferent to the legal structure of the contract of sale. Yet *inter alia*, the statute enacted that when the contract between the buyer and seller was formally executed, the seller's
certain and true ownership had to be proved by the neighbours, thus
creating a very considerable breach in the concept of sale as a consensual contract.[6] One can also add the law of the Emperor Justin I
of A.D. 520–3 which permitted a penitent actress to be rehabilitated:
inter alia she could apply for an imperial grant of full marriage
privileges, whereupon the highest aristocrat could marry her without
stain.[7] The real purpose of the law was to permit Justin's nephew,
the future Emperor Justinian to marry Theodora. Significantly both
the Statute of Uses and the law of Justin have a preamble stressing
the general good which is intended by the law.[8] (We do not have the
wording of the *senatus consultum Claudianum*.)

Similarly, once draft legislation is prepared it may fail to pass the legislature simply because of pressure of business. This is especially clear for modern times and there are so many instances for contemporary Britain that the point does not have to be pursued.[9] An example which has already come up in this volume may be mentioned. As a result of the Porter Committee's report on defamation, the Defamation Bill in 1952 contained as clause 11 a provision that the defendant in order to mitigate damages could bring forward facts relevant to the plaintiff's character. To finish the Third Reading of the Bill on the due date this clause was dropped. *Plato Films Ltd. v. Speidel* of 1961 showed how needed such a clause was, and hence the Freedom of Publication Bill was introduced in 1966. It never became law; no time was ever found for the Second Reading. The Faulks Committee recommendation of a reform along similar lines has, of course, not yet been acted on.[10] As for other systems, no Scot needs to be told how peculiarly difficult it is for a reform of Scots private law to pass the United Kingdom parliament.

Moreover, once a draft bill is laid before the legislature amendments of various types may be accepted and the resulting legislation may correspond to the wishes of no one and be not even a satisfactory compromise. Then that law may continue in existence for centuries.

Legislation – even on private law – is very often a 'gut reaction', an immediate, strong response to some particular event. The danger here is not that the legislation fails to correspond to the immediate wishes of the people, but that over-reaction can entail harmful consequences as well, and that, legislation being what it is, the situation may never be put right. Thus, it seems that in the first century A.D. a gentleman called Macedo, a son in the *potestas* of his father, was in the grip of moneylenders. To pay off his debts he needed to inherit from his father, to inherit he killed his father. The consequence was the *senatusconsultum Macedonianum* which decreed that a person who lent money to a *filiusfamilias* could not sue for its return even when the son became independent of paternal power.[11] The *senatusconsultum* was never repealed despite the commercial inconvenience of the rule. Yet it could not have been a frequent fear that a son would kill his father in order to pay off his debts. Another Roman example would be the abolition of *nexum* by the *lex Poetilia* of 326, or, more likely 313 B.C.[12] *Nexum* was in effect a form of security in which a Roman pledged himself or a son until a debt should be repaid. *Nexum* could be used in various ways and it had advantages for the needy Roman. For instance, the borrower could continue in *de facto* liberty to work his land without having to hand over any of his precious possessions to the creditor for security. The creditor could be well content, because he had a strong security which could easily be enforced in the event of non-payment.[13] But *nexum* was open to abuse by creditors. According to Roman tradition the cause of the *lex Poetilia* was the attempted rape or seduction of a handsome young *nexus* by the creditor.[14] *Nexum* was never reestablished, and no equivalent form of security was put in its place. The advantages of self-pledge in an early agricultural society were needlessly lost. For England it is hard to pass over a passage from A. V. Dicey (even though it does not really concern private law):

> The Money-lenders Act, 1900, again, may well be called an Act for the suppression of Isaac Gordon, since it was to a great extent the outcome of indignation against the rapacity and cruelty of that particular usurer. But this Act, though produced by temporary feeling, not only revives the usury laws, but gives expression and authority to beliefs supposed to have been confuted by reason.[15]

The description of a 'gut reaction' also fits many private member's bills in the U.K.

Finally in a world in which small numbers of people may openly organise themselves to operate – in many cases very successfully – as a pressure group, it scarcely needs to be said that often legislation is and has been the result of pressure from overt or hidden groups.[16] Clearly a law may result which is beneficial to the group but does not conform to what society as a whole needs or wants. If little is said about this phenomenon here it is only because it is so obvious and well recognised.

Yet it should be stressed that most statutes concerning private law are in line with at least what is conceived to be the interest of society or the rulers. Without doubt one would learn a great deal about the nature of a society, its needs and its wishes, from looking at its legislation.[17] What must be emphasised for an understanding of law in society is the great extent to which private law is left unaltered even though it is out of step with desires or needs. It is fascinating that to please the Emperor the *senatusconsultum Claudianum* permitted marriage with a brother's daughter, but not with a sister's daughter. But it is in the highest degree much more significant that no alteration occurred either to allow or prohibit marriage with any niece for three centuries.

Everywhere it is necessary for the law to be tested and interpreted, a function which for the most part is not, and in the nature

of things usually cannot be, left to the legislature. These interpreters of the law tend to form a separate group – the jurists of
ancient Rome, the academic legal writers of pre-codified Europe,
the judges in England.[18] In strict theory they may in some instances
be regarded simply as 'finders of the law', but in practice they will
also be 'makers of the law'. The more the legislative body fails to
keep law in step with society, the more the law-making function will
devolve on these interpreters of the law. But they never have the
freedom to innovate which the legislature has.[19] However much the
legislature may leave the task of keeping the law up to date to the
interpreters, it never gives them power directly to make radical
changes. Scarman, discussing the problem of reform in contemporary
England says:[20]

> The courts have the technical learning most assuredly; the social
> awareness perhaps; but neither the opportunity nor the power to
> tackle the job systematically.

The whole Western concept of legal argument is the result of this
very restricted freedom given to the interpreters. Certain types of
argument become respectable and acceptable, others do not. We
need not consider the nature of legal argument here. But what has
to be said is that – in general – the interpreter, whether he is concerned with an abstract rule or a particular case, must in the main
justify his proposition with arguments from analogy with existing
legal rules in a similar context or from authority whether precedents
from his own system or an opinion expressed in another system
which is deemed worthy of respect. These arguments must be in
terms acceptable within the system and they are backward-looking.
It may well be that in the individual situation the interpreter is
being most radical, but that cannot, on the whole, appear explicitly
on the record. He will, for instance, use a false analogy or (deliberately) misinterpret foreign authority.[21] The interpreter may have
made up his mind as to what the decision should be, and the arguments may be nothing more than a false justification. Nonetheless,
the fact that such are the arguments which are used helps to create a
climate of opinion where conservative tendencies among interpreters
are further strengthened. Dicey stresses that an inherent defect of
what he calls 'judicial legislation' is that the progress of reform is
slow.[22] In addition it is a common feeling among lawyers including
judges that it is not their business to be constructive but to operate
the law as it is.[23]

Judges, moreover, when they do take liberty to decide overtly on
policy grounds are as much subject to 'gut reactions' as legislators;

and both seem to have the greatest difficulty in sticking consistently to any policy. Thus, England is at present engaged in introducing at very considerable expense a system of compulsory registration of title. At the same time the courts are engaged in multiplying equitable interests which arise by implication, by transactions which take place off the register, and in one field, that of husband and wife, the legislature has actually encouraged this process.[24] So again, it has recently been decided that if I allow my man of business to prepare papers for my signature, and sign a deed without reading it, this will be an effective conveyance to a third party if I am found to have been negligent.[25] If on the other hand I knowingly convey away my property, on the assurance that this is a pure formality, for the sake of more convenient management, this is a good trust in my favour, which I may enforce against an innocent third party who has acquired the property for value, if he can be fixed with constructive notice – and the present tendency is to extend the doctrine of constructive notice very widely.[26] (Constructive notice is where knowledge of the fact is assumed from the surrounding circumstances.)

One striking characteristic of the interpreters, both as individuals and as a group, is a tendency to restrict the area of their interest. Not all law seems to attract their attention and whole fields are left uncultivated. Which fields these are vary from place to place and time to time and will depend on particular social factors. For much of Roman history the most obvious field of neglect by the jurists was criminal law, which, in consequence never approached the pitch of excellence of private law.[27] In the later nineteenth and the twentieth century, English judges have shown reluctance to involve their courts in aspects of the 'welfare state'. Moreover, in matters clearly within their competence such as regulation of business monopolies they have been rather unwilling to make policy decisions. They have not always in fact made full use of their powers of law making.[28] Legal philosophers of the dominant analytical school, prefer to exclude from enquiry international law and primitive law.[29]

Yet another characteristic of lawyers is to want legal rules with which they feel at ease. Sensible or practical or even just results may often seem somehow improper unless they can be regarded as fitting into the existing legal structure. Thus, L. C. B. Gower[30] calls attention to the difficulties encountered by the Law Commissions in England and Scotland in unifying the law of contract, even when both teams were agreed on results. Both sides wished that in certain circumstances a unilateral promise not supported by consideration should be enforceable as indeed is already the case. Gower was ready to define contract so that the term would include such a promise.

But his Scottish opposite number could not agree to this: a *pollicitatio* could not be a contract. So clear is this characteristic that Friedrich Engels made good use of it. From his own point of view he argued that in a modern state where division of labour had made professional lawyers necessary, law strives for an internally coherent expression which will detract from law corresponding to the general economic condition and from a code of law being 'the blunt, unmitigated, unadulterated expression of the domination of a class'.[31]

The power of the interpreters to reform the law or keep it static is, despite everything, considerable. These interpreters will form a small group within a society – indeed, a small group even among lawyers – and their views need not correspond to society as a whole. Loyalty to the group or to a wider circle of lawyers may deform the law further.[32]

As Savigny well knew,[33] the role of lawyers is central to legal development. The credit for legal progress must largely be given to them. Yet is should be stressed that often lawyers' own financial interests or – a different matter – their professional outlook will distort the law from what is desirable for the rest of society. Each group of lawyers will have its own interests, and when these protected interests are added together a formidable picture of professional resistance may emerge especially since one group of lawyers will not press for a reform which is contrary to the financial advantage of another group. To give a few examples, The English common lawyers and common law judges benefited from Henry VIII's Statute of Uses. Chancery lawyers were not prominent in attacking the abuses which lined their pockets and were the target of Charles Dickens' *Bleak House*. Present day English barristers and Scottish advocates have no contractual relationship with their clients hence they cannot be sued by them for breach of contract.[34] In turn, it is true, the barristers cannot sue for payment of fees; but the solicitors are responsible for paying their fees, and the solicitors can sue the clients. Little attempt is made to improve the legal rights of the clients. The Scottish Faculty of Advocates would not, I believe, welcome any simplification of divorce law which might enable cases to be heard in courts below the Court of Session where they have exclusive right of being heard. Solicitors in both jurisdictions have not been anxious to have conveyancing reformed; and in England where the solicitors' monopoly has been under attack the Law Society has been active in protecting it.[35] The Scottish Law Commissioners and academics, as we have seen, are more anxious than the solicitors' professional organisation to have the law in what they see as a satisfactory systematic state and are less concerned with the practical results. Academic ideas lead to the neglect of certain aspects of law in Law Faculty syllabuses, thus distorting the view presented to future practitioners.[36]

The very particular part played by legal scaffolding should be stressed. Initially it operates to moderate – not cure or remove – the divergence. But in the process it makes the law more complicated and remote from the understanding of the ordinary citizen. By the complexities which it introduces it makes it much more difficult to see the wood from the trees, and to know what form the improvements should take. The complexities serve to give lawyers a pride in the technicalities of their craft, to foster the feeling that lawyers are a race apart and that law cannot be understood or appreciated by others. The scaffolding focuses the lawyers' attention and admiration on the skill involved in winning a particular suit, and diverts that attention from the worthiness of the suit. Successful lawyers come to enjoy the technicalities for their own sake. Concurrently the lawyers' delight in and understanding of the technicalities make others – the public at large as well as legislators who lack a legal training – feel more hesitant in asking for change.

A word should be said about the Praetor's Edict in Rome and the Chancellor's Equity jurisdiction in England. Both represent attempts to supplement law making by the legislatures and the law interpreters. The Edict is more akin to legislation, Equity is more like other court decisions. Both were remarkably successful in modernising the law, and bringing it more into step with the needs and wishes of society. Neither was anything like completely successful, or the chapters in this book on Roman and English law could never have been written. These chapters took into full account the contribution of praetorian law and equity, and found, notwithstanding, that law to a very considerable extent did not meet the needs or wishes of society.[37]

Naturally this book stresses the divergences. Yet on the other side I should like to emphasise that it can happen first that a person or body with legislative power makes a new ruling for purely administrative purposes, secondly that the legal ruling may be contrary to all established legal principle, thirdly that the lawyers want to feel at ease with the ruling and that nonetheless the result can only be described as a notable social and legal advance. Let me give one illustration.

Throughout the Roman Republic only a person free from paternal power could own property. It was common, though, as we have seen for a *paterfamilias* to allow a son (and indeed slaves as well) to hold a fund called the *peculium* with which within particular limits he could trade, though not make a gift without the father's consent. The son, of course, could not make a will since the *peculium* was not his property. Such was the legal position until Augustus, for the first time in Roman history, made a breach in the idea that all proprietary rights belonged to those independent of power. Augustus' innovation was, as David Daube has emphasised,[38] very limited in extent, and there is no controversy over the nature of the reform. He permitted soldier *filiifamiliarum* to make a will of what they acquired in camp. This right ended when the *filius* ceased to be a soldier. The Emperor Hadrian extended the right also to veterans.[39] There is no indication that Augustus made any further innovations in the law in this context.

Augustus' ruling is so clear that, so far as I am aware, it appears to have passed unnoticed that Augustus was not in the slightest concerned with legal principle and in fact created a legal monstrosity. To whom did the military acquisitions belong while the *filius* was still a soldier and alive? Augustus seems not to have dealt with this point. If we say they belonged to the *pater* – as they certainly seem to have done when the son's military service was over – we must concede that it is bizarre that the son by will could transfer ownership of something he himself did not own. Moreover, if these acquisitions belonged to the *pater* they would not necessarily by any means fall within the son's *peculium*. The son might not have been granted a *peculium*. Even if he had been, it would depend on the nature of the grant whether acquisitions of this kind were included. By what legal right then, could the son deal with his military acquisitions? If we say the acquisitions did belong to the *filius* then how did it happen that he apparently lost ownership automatically when he was discharged?

What the practical situation was before Augustus' ruling is easy to reconstruct. The *filius*, far from home and in military surroundings. would do with his pay and his booty whatever he wanted. The father would have no control.[40] If the son died on service the military authorities would try to ensure that whatever belonged to the *filius* would be sent home to his father. But a difficult situation would arise if the *filius* had indicated to his comrades his wishes that someone other than the father should inherit from him. A conflict, not easy to resolve, would arise between military group loyalty and superiors' concern for their officers and men on the one hand and the civil law on the other. Augustus' constitution was intended to resolve this conflict. It did so neatly, but at the expense of legal principle.

Augustus' ruling is obviously a privilege granted to the soldiers. But why did he not regulate the status of military acquisitions for the lifetime of the *filius*? And why was the right of testation to end with the soldier's discharge? These questions prompt us to look for the motive which inspired the exact scope of the constitution. Did Augustus intend to benefit the *filius* soldier's comrades in arms or a woman with whom he had formed an attachment? The evidence suggests, I submit, that no clear intention to bestow benefits was in Augustus' mind. If he had thought primarily of the well-being, psychical or material, of the soldier *filius*, his comrades in arms or his woman, then Augustus would have considered the situation more in the round, and the *constitutio* would have declared that during his service a soldier *filius* could treat his military acquisitions as his own personal property and even leave them by will. The very restricted scope of the constitution and the legal monstrosity which it created is explicable only on the basis that Augustus' attention was riveted on the outstanding practical problem which caused administrative difficulties. Augustus' concern was easy administration rather than benevolence – even politically motivated – towards his troops.

This constitution of Augustus was the first step towards the creation of that very satisfactory institution, the *peculium castrense*, a fund which the soldier or veteran *filius* could treat virtually as if he were owner. Its success is famous and we need not here trace the steps by which it was incorporated into the general legal framework. It is enough to observe that later jurists held that while the soldier lived he could deal as a *paterfamilias* with what he acquired in and by means of his service,[41] and that he had the rights of action of a *paterfamilias* to protect such acquisitions.[42]

I should like to end this chapter on a very different note, by considering two possible objections to my general thesis. It might be argued that the whole approach is wrong, that one should proceed from the system as a whole and not from individual instances and institutions. If one did that, it might be suggested, then one would see that systems of private law do correspond to the needs and wishes of the society or to the will of the ruling élite. It might be argued that there is a fundamental difference between a sociological approach and a legal approach (such as mine might be presumed to be). Sociology, it might be said, is concerned with the typical (and types may be blurred at the edges), law with the marginal. For the sociologist, a forest would not cease to be green because of the presence of a single copperbeech; the lawyer would focus his attention on the copperbeech and devalue the forest's greenness. To such an argument I would reply in the first instance that particularly in the case of Roman law we have looked at a great deal of the whole system and have found that it failed to meet needs and desires, and that this divergence must have been obvious to the Romans. It would be easy, I believe, to take other branches of Roman private law and show an equally great divergence. In the case of English law we have examined in some detail the law of land tenure, land registration and defamation, all apparently fundamental matters for our happiness and well-being, and found English law, too, had greatly diverged from the needs of society. We have observed glaring defects in recent criminal law and en passant noted Mr. Commissioner Gower's opinion that the law of contract had failed to adapt itself to changing conditions. Secondly it should be stressed that it has never been my intention to claim that there is no connection between private law and the society in which it operates. I firmly believe that some relationship does exist. It would be absurd to maintain that at no point does private law meet the needs or wishes of its society or the ruling élite. Obviously one would expect that a country like South Africa would not accept as valid marriage between persons of different race. And that Catholic Ireland would not permit divorce. Moreover one would expect some general correlation though it does not appear easy to formulate what it is. (I should add that some kind of general correlation would in no sense be hostile to the thesis in this book). In part the correlation is a negative one: some rules will not be tolerable in a given society. Thirdly, if proceeding from the system as a whole was the correct approach and proceeding from individual instances and institutions was not we would expect – what in fact is not the case – that societies which had a relatively similar legal system would be relatively like one another in politics, economics and social *mores*, those which had a relatively different legal system would likewise differ more in these regards. If this approach were sound we would expect Germany to be more like Greece or Japan in social, economic, political and moral attitudes and less like Britain. The province of Quebec would be more like France and less like Ontario.

The second possible objection is that in considering the appropriateness of legal rules for the society it may be thought wrong to discuss legal rules in isolation, that they should be considered as but one weapon in a whole battery of means of social control; organised religion, economic conditions, widely-held ideas of morality. If legal rules, it might be urged, were considered in the whole context of means of social control, then it would emerge that much of what may appear as divergence between law and society is irrelevant, because society or its rulers are bypassing law and using one of these other means of control. The observation of the power of other means of control has, of course, force. But I do not believe that the argument affects my thesis to any significant extent. I have, above all, in the preceding chapters sought to give examples where the disadvantages of the legal rules were not seriously modified by other means of social control. Thus the defects in Roman contract law – such as the need for a stipulation if a consensual contract of sale was to be satisfactory to the buyer – or in English land tenure and registration or in the law of defamation, do not appear any less if one takes note of other possible means of social control. How can religious ideas etc. modify the working of the legal rules which distinguished between manifest theft and non-manifest theft? Certainly ethical and religious beliefs could modify the working of *patria potestas*, but I concentrated on aspects of that institution which were not much affected, such as the inability of a person in power to own property, hence his incapacity to make a will or even to have property which on his death would pass under the rules of intestate succession. The very complex legal rules which developed to give someone who contracted with a person in power some legal protection in certain defined circumstances themselves indicate that it was not expected that other forms of social control would be effective against the head of the family for the benefit of the contracting party in these or in other circumstances.

A distinction is often drawn, reasonably, between 'law in action' and 'law in books' the latter scarcely counting as living law. Obviously in a work of the present kind what matters most is 'law in action'. If the only law out of step with society was that 'in books' the observation of it would have little social significance. I have tried to show that 'law in action' frequently diverges from the needs and desires of society. Yet one should not altogether discount 'law in books'. Unless one defines the term as law which is totally ignored in practice or which never appears in a legal issue, weak 'law in books' can make the law more difficult to grasp, obscure the path of reform, drive parties to unnecessarily expensive behaviour.

On a different level it might further be charged that I have not looked at law in the round; that I should also have discussed administrative law, social welfare law, evidence and procedure and the workings of the court; that only when that is done, can one ask how far law is out of step with society. Such a charge would make me very uneasy. And yet my narrow focus is deliberate. My concern has been to establish whether rules of substantive private law are or are not in step with the needs and desires of the society; whether the factors which cause the rules of private law to develop are sufficiently strong and in tune with the needs of society or of the ruling class to enable private law to keep reasonable pace. The answer to both counts is negative.

Notes

1. See, e.g. *The German Civil Code* translated with an introduction by I. S. Forrester, S. L. Goven, H. M. Ilgen (Amsterdam, North Holland Publishing Co. 1975), p. xiv.
2. See Watson, *Law Making*, pp. 95ff.
3. See for a detailed history, B. H. Lee, *Divorce Law Reform in England* (London, Peter Owen, 1974).
4. See supra, pp. 37ff.
5. See supra, pp. 91f.
6. *Vaticana Fragmenta* 35; *Codex Theodosianus*, 3.1.2. See, e.g. E. Levy, *West Roman Vulgar Law, The Law of Property* (Philadelphia, American Philosophical Society, 1951), pp. 128f; V. Arangio-Ruiz, *La compravendita in diritto romano*, 2nd edit. (Naples, Jovene, 1956), pp. 94f; C. Dupont, 'La vente dans les constitutions de Constantin', *RIDA* 2 (1955), pp. 237ff at pp. 238ff.
7. C.5.4.23: on the full scope and purpose of the law see D. Daube, 'The Marriage of Justinian and Theodora. Legal and Theological Reflections', *Catholic University of America Law Review* 16 (1967), pp. 380ff.
8. The Statute of Uses is conveniently printed in L. E. Digby, *Introduction to the History of the Law of Real Property* (Oxford, Clarendon Press, 1876), pp. 312ff.
9. See, e.g. L. Scarman, *Law Reform, The New Pattern* (London, Routledge & Kegan Paul, 1968), p. 8.
10. For difficulties in getting private law bills through Parliament see also B. H. Lee, *Divorce Law Reform.*
11. See D. Daube, 'Did Macedo Kill his Father?' *ZSS* 65 (1947), pp. 261ff.
12. See Watson, *Law Making*, pp. 6ff.
13. See Watson, *Rome of the XII Tables*, pp. 111ff.
14. Livy, 8.28.
15. *Law and Public Opinion*, p. 45. Dicey also refers to the severe Garotters Act, 1863 (chapter 44) passed because an M.P. had been garotted.
16. See, e.g. Farrar, *Law Reform*, pp. 68ff.
17. See, e.g. Dicey, *Law and Public Opinion, passim.*
18. See in general J. P. Dawson, *The Oracles of the Law* (Ann Arbor, University of Michigan Law School, 1968).
19. See, e.g. Dicey, *Law and Public Opinion*, pp. 166f, on the reforms of Lord Mansfield. I am not here including as interpreters of the law

the Praetors of Rome or the Chancellors of England. They did, of course, have very considerable freedom to innovate.

20. *Law Reform*, p. 8.
21. For free use of Roman authority see e.g. Watson, *Legal Transplants*, pp. 57ff.
22. *Law and Public Opinion*, pp. 395ff. But it is worth noting that in the United States, by what is known as the 'Brandeis brief', counsel is permitted to produce evidence from the social sciences to show the probable result of legislation when the constitutionality of that legislation is being attacked: *Muller v. Oregon* (1908), 208 U.S. 412; see, e.g. J. Home, *Social Dimensions of Law and Justice* (London, Stevens, 1966), p. 48, n150.
23. See, e.g. Lord Macmillan in *Reed v. Lyons* [1947] A.C. 156 at p. 175; G. Sawer, *Law in Society* (Oxford, Clarendon Press, 1965), pp. 18f, especially for the quotations from Sir Owen Dixon.
24. Matrimonial Proceedings and Property Act 1970, s. 37.
25. *Saunders v. Anglican Building Society*, 1971 A.C. 1004.
26. *Hodgson v. Marks*, 1971 2 All E.R. 684.
27. See, e.g. J. A. C. Thomas, 'The Development of Roman Criminal Law', *LQR* 79 (1963), pp. 224ff.
28. See. e.g. B. Abel-Smith and R. Stevens, *Lawyers and the Courts* (London, Heinemann, 1967), especially chapters 4, 5 and 11.
29. See H. L. A. Hart, *The Concept of Law* (Oxford, Clarendon Press, 1961), pp. 3ff.
30. 'Reflections on Law Reform', *University of Toronto Law Journal* 23 (1973), pp. 257ff, at p. 264.
31. Letter to C. Schmidt, dated October 27, 1890 (published in e.g. Marx, Engels, *Selected Works* (London, Lawrence & Wishart, 1968), pp. 684ff).
32. Thus Dicey; 'But whilst our tribunals, or the judges of whom they are composed, are swayed by the prevailing beliefs of a particular time, they are also guided by professional opinions and ways of thinking which are, to a certain extent, independent of and possibly opposed to the general tone of public opinion. The judges are the heads of the legal profession. They have acquired the intellectual and the moral tone of English lawyers. They are for the most part persons of a conservative disposition. They are in no way dependent for their emoluments, dignity, or reputation upon the favour of the electors, or even of Ministers who represent in the long run the wishes of the electorate. Hence judicial legislation will be often marked by certain characteristics rarely to be found in Acts of Parliament', *Law and Public Opinion*, pp. 364.
33. *Vom Beruf unsrer Zeit für Gesetzgebung und Rechtswissenschaft*, 3rd edit. (Heidelberg, Mohr, 1840), pp. 7f.
34. In restricted circumstances, a barrister can be sued for negligence: see Salmond, *Law of Torts*, 16th edit. by R. F. V. Heuston (London,

Sweet & Maxwell, 1973). pp. 210f; Winfield and Jolowicz, *Tort*, 10th edit. by W. V. H. Rogers (London, Sweet & Maxwell, 1975), p. 63.

35. See for instance the splendid case reported in *The Times* for January 3, 1976, p. 3 and the article, p. 13. A person, whose company had previously been prosecuted for conveying property without the services of a solicitor, brought a private prosecution in the magistrates' court against a clerk who had prepared conveyances for a firm of solicitors. The magistrates held that no offence is committed when solicitors leave conveyancing work to their clerks. The Law Society's solicitors instructed leading counsel and a junior counsel for the defence. Costs were awarded against the prosecutor who estimated they would be about £1,500. The maximum penalty for the offence charged is a fine of £50.

36. See Watson, *Legal Transplants*, pp. 39ff. One of the most interesting distortions by academics occurs, I believe, in the U.S.A. The emphasis on the 'case method' (partly resulting from the influence of the Realists) stresses the marginal more than the typical, and legal principles tend to be underrated. The training is geared to the trial lawyer rather than the legal adviser.

37. Nothing need be said here about legal changes which are unfortunate because of a lack of understanding by the law maker.

38. *Roman Law, Linguistic, Social, and Philosophical Aspects* (Edinburgh, Edinburgh University Press, 1969), pp. 76f.

39. *Ulp. Epit.* 20.10; J.2.12pr.

40. See Daube, *loc. cit.*

41. D.14.6.2 (Ulpian *64 ad ed.*); 49.17.12 (Papinian *14 quaest.*).

42. D.49.17.4 (Tertullian *sing. castr. pec.*). For all questions on the *peculium castrense* see above all F. La Rosa, *I Peculii speciali in diritto romano* (Milan, Giuffrè, 1953). Unfortunately her account is weak in the historical development.

Chapter 11

SOME CONCLUSIONS

The general argument of this book has been, it will be recalled, not that private law fails to mirror the needs and desires of society or its ruling élite, but that to a very considerable extent law is out of step with such needs and desires.[1] This divergence, it has been maintained, is so great that none of the theories of the development of law or the relationship between law and society are acceptable even though each, or at least some, may contain much accurate observation. If the argument is correct various conclusions follow.

The first conclusion must simply be that there does not exist a close, inherent, necessary relationship between existing rules of law and the society in which they operate. Law is not in any mystical sense 'the spirit of the people'. Many rules are contrary to the ethos of society, its needs and desires, and do not correspond to the interests or wishes of the ruling élite. Moreover, when we take into account the longevity of legal rules and the frequency of transplants we see that usually legal rules were not created for the society in which they now operate.[2] It follows from this that in many cases legal rules are equally at home in many places. Even some of the most particular rules will equally suit a similar or different environment. Different reasons will favour the acceptance of the same rule in several jurisdictions. Legal rules tend to be general in the sense that they exist in and should operate for a community of people from different backgrounds living in different geographical, economic and social circumstances.

A second conclusion is that in developed society at least law does not emerge easily from society. As society grows, as institutions are created to cope with changes, then some might think, as Friedrich von Savigny argued,[3] that law would keep in step (or perhaps be only slightly behind), that law would spontaneously issue forth from some source such as national consciousness. This is far from the truth. It is difficult for legal rules which correspond to the needs and wishes of the society to come into being. (I am not talking here of the intellectual difficulty in perceiving the changes in the law which would be beneficial, since we have been concerned throughout with the slowness of change once the benefits of change have become apparent.) Reform requires a great effort. Such was also the opinion of Rudolf von Ihering who saw changes in law as a battle in which it was not weight of arguments but the proportion of power which could be wielded by the opposing parties which decided the issue.

> Only in this way can it be explained how institutions, over whose head public opinion has long since broken its staff, often manage to live on. So they do, yet it is not the *vis inertiae* which preserves their existence, but the force of the resistance made by those interests that are concerned in their preservation.[4]

The argument in this book does not wholly support Ihering's theory. The force of inertia is very relevant to keeping institutions and rules alive when their unsatisfactory nature has been revealed. The force of inertia, it will be recalled, is often successful because the body or person who has legislative power has other concerns, the interpreters of the law have limited power, and legal scaffolding for a variety of reasons operates to hide the need.[5] Inertia operates both to prevent a legal rule from developing to a satisfactory state and to inhibit change when society changes.

Eugen Ehrlich wished to sum up his book, *Fundamental Principles of the Sociology of Law*,[6] in one sentence in the foreword:

> At the present as well as at any other time, the center of gravity of legal development lies not in legislation, nor in juristic science, nor in judicial decision, but in society itself.

But one must not overlook the forces of inaction. I very much doubt if one could claim that the centre of gravity of rules of private law lies in the existing society itself. Ehrlich also stressed that what he called 'state law' lags behind only too often. But this 'rigid immobile state law' he contrasts with 'the unceasing development of the social law'.[7] 'Social law' in the sense in which he uses the term seems to mean how people do act. It includes what other scholars would exclude altogether from the concept of law, namely rights and duties emanating from social and moral consciousness but with no legal enforcement, and transactions where the parties make their own arrangements which a court will enforce even though the terms are not those standardised by the law, e.g. contracts imposing a different standard of care, or excluding liability or modifying the moment of transfer of risk. With regard to this second element of 'social law' it is only too often the case – as many of the examples in this volume show – that the parties' legal position cannot be altered by their agreement.

The third conclusion – perhaps the most startling and certainly one which informs all others – is that the great extent of the divergence is not readily apparent. If it had been, much attention would be focused on it, theories would take it more into account. This can only mean that the role of private law rules in the well-being of the state, in the prosperity of merchants, in the happiness of individuals, is greatly exaggerated by lawyers and legal theorists.[8] One should not, of course, cynically ignore the pain which may be caused by, for instance, bad divorce law. But the truth seems to be that at any time only a relatively very small number of people actually suffer badly from a legal rule being out of step,[9] and are conscious that their misery could be alleviated by a change in the law.

The divergence has at times been stressed. Jeremy Bentham, above all, never tired of pointing out how unsuitable much of English law was for the society as a whole.[10] His standpoint was rather different from ours, and he was not directly interested in the question whether the legal rules as they each existed were in harmony with the interests of the ruling élite. He was fully aware that much of English law as it was in his day could be explained only by its history and not by its existing utility, and his followers were responsible for a very great deal of the law reform of the nineteenth century.[11] In the present context one of the most interesting things is that, despite the efforts and influence of Bentham, the realisation of the divergences – which still continue – dimmed.[12]

Moreover, except where law reform is intended to be in advance of society, to mould society's views, every demand for law reform is a recognition that law has come to diverge from society. Without the recognition of the fact of divergence, law could scarcely evolve.[13] What I have wanted to emphasise is rather that as a general rule there is a much less intimate connection between society and its rules of private law than is usually thought.

Fourthly, the present shape of a rule of private law has more to do with history than with the present structure of society. 'History' here is used in the widest possible sense: history of the nation, its feuds, intellectual contacts, past social, economic and political conditions and its languages; history of legal life, the activity of the legislature, powers of the interpreters of law, energy and opinions of individual lawyers such as Grotius or Blackstone; history which is not woven into the general fabric of society, random events which affect a powerful individual or produce a more general 'gut reaction'. All this means, of course, that to have any real understanding of a legal rule, its scope, purpose, utility and suitability, one must know its history. This in turn means that if we want to have a legal rule suited to our needs we must in many instances cleanse it from its history, take it right away from our existing tradition. 'Law can only rejuvenate itself by clearing away its own past' says Jhering.[14] The existing dependence of law on its own past history and what had to be done for reform were admirably described by Oliver Wendell Holmes at the end of last century in his famous paper, 'The Path of the Law'.[15] But not everyone would agree with this diagnosis. Thus, P. S. Atiyah writes:[16]

> It will be seen from the absence of any historical introduction that I do not share the commonly expressed belief that the law of contract cannot be understood without a knowledge of its history stretching back to the Middle Ages or even beyond. On the contrary, I strongly believe that it is virtually impossible to understand the history of this subject without a knowledge of the modern law, and I do not think so ill of the modern law as to believe that it cannot be reduced to a reasonably coherent set of principles, capable of comprehension on their own.

Fifthly, neither the ruling élite nor society in general has usually been too concerned about the state of private law. There is surprising tolerance of inappropriate law, both a willingness and ability to put up with much which is clearly unsatisfactory. In the main the legislative élite has been prepared to give control over development to the interpreters of the law without allowing them the power to make sufficient changes. Generally society does not put much pressure on the legislature for reform. When a small group wishes the law changed this seldom seems to arouse society to defend the status quo. (It may do so, of course. Thus, when legislation was proposed to permit marriage with a deceased wife's sister there was in 1883 a flood of pamphlets in England to defend the existing position.[17] Legislation to that effect was passed only in 1907.) It would seem that much of private law has a content which is not of sufficient political, social, economic or moral importance, to generate excitement. Here one should add that if, as Ihering maintains, legal rules have to be fought for and legal improvements result from battle, then the fight for change is in general not vigorous enough.

There is a case to be made out for the proposition that it would be beneficial to have a law making body intermediate between the courts and the legislature; with greater and more systematic powers of law making than courts have, but not subject to the political pressures experienced by legislatures.

Jurists often write as if it is the speed of change – technological even more than social – in modern life which causes the divergence between private law and society. Law, it is said, cannot, or does not, keep pace.[18] No doubt the speed of social and technological change does make the problem more acute (though less in the field of private law than elsewhere). But we have seen that in earlier, slower-moving, pre-industrialised societies, there were serious well-known legal deficiencies which continued for centuries. The sixth conclusion is therefore that the root cause of divergence is not to be sought in the idea that society changes and that law responds, hence that there must be a small time-lag before law catches up.

Seventhly, if so much of law is badly out of step yet is accepted, then it seems likely that many other legal rules which are not badly out of step will also not represent in any convincing way the particular wishes or needs of society. This is not, strictly speaking, a conclusion since it does not follow from the arguments of the preceding pages. But the preceding arguments do make the statement plausible, and it is useful to set it down. The statement could, I believe, be easily verified. It would seem that in many cases it will not matter greatly to society whether the law adopts solution A or solution B; the choice is socially neutral.[19]

If society is in many situations of private law not greatly concerned with the moral, economic or social aspects of the matter, why does it bother to pass laws in such areas or have expensive and complicated legal proceedings? The answer is to avoid disputes or resolve them peacefully. This brings us to the eighth conclusion that the essential, inescapable function of a rule of private law is to help in avoiding or settling conflicts.[20] The rule may also have, but need not have, the function of resolving a dispute for the moral, social or economic well-being of the society. Society's essential stake in rules of private law is the avoidance or peaceful resolving of conflicts. This can occur only if formal justice is applied between the parties to a dispute; both sides must be given an equal chance to put their case, there should be no decision *ad hominem*, similar situations should be judged alike, and so on.[21]

Yet as has been emphasised several times before in this volume, there must be some relationship between the needs and desires of society and its legal rules. The rules must have a connection with the society in some way and to some extent. But this relationship seems impossible to define, perhaps because it varies from state to state and from one area of law to another. As some of the examples discussed in previous chapters show, the relationship cannot be expressed by saying that a legal rule will cease to exist if it deviates beyond a certain degree of unsatisfactoriness for society.

One approach to the relationship might be by examining the legal changes which are made. The forces of inertia are so great that each time a legal change is made society reveals something important about itself. The changes should be examined from the perspective both of the rule or principle or proposition which is created and of that which is abrogated. The latter viewpoint which is easily overlooked is at times especially significant since it not infrequently happens that the concern is more to abolish an existing rule than to introduce a particular reform.

But even with this approach the *substance* of the rule may reveal less about the wishes or needs of the society or its ruling class than one might hope. Thus, as we have seen, the *senatusconsultum* in the reign of Claudius permitting marriage with a brother's daughter does not show that the senators had strong views on degrees of relationship as a bar to marriage. Rather, what it reveals is that senators wished to please the Emperor. The Statute of Uses does not tell us that the King in Parliament felt that the incipient law of trusts would disfigure the land law; but only that Henry desperately needed money, and that Parliament was not strong enough to resist this device to get one. Again, adoption of a foreign rule does not inevitably show that after proper consideration of all known options this rule was thought the most suitable. It may do so in particular cases, but need not. Thus, the general respect for the foreign source, the language in which it is written and the general accessibility of the foreign law, the attitude of those particularly engaged in shaping the law to law from elsewhere, may all determine the final outcome. When one knows all the surrounding circumstances one can see the relationship between a new legal rule and its society. But the relationship is by no means simply that the *proposition* of law must be inherently suitable for the society or its rulers.

At this stage there is one thing I should like to make explicit. Throughout I have been talking about legal *rules*, and not about how decisions are reached by the courts – though occasionally judicial reasoning on law has slipped in – or how the legal system actually works. What I have had to say should be treated independently of the propositions of Legal Realists or of the insights of students of Sociology of Law. Though I have no intention of investigating the subject here, yet the views of Realists and sociologists of law are very *à propos*.

Thus, the argument has been, in history as a whole there has been considerable divergence between the rules of private law and the needs and desires of society. It has not been, and cannot be, claimed that the divergence cannot be diminished. Otherwise there would be little point in contemplating law reform. Indeed, legal evolution would otherwise be virtually unthinkable. Theoretically it should be possible to make the legal rules coincide with the needs and desires of society. To some extent it is a question of allocating sufficient resources. I have drawn conclusions, yet have not touched upon one of the major features of many modern systems, namely codes. The reason is that from the perspective of this study, codification complicates the issue. Codes in the modern world, whatever else they may be, should be seen as a step towards deliberately rationalising the law. The same is true of the setting up of permanent bodies with the duty of considering law reform, such as the Law Commission in England or the Scottish Law Commission. Within the framework of this book it would be difficult to discuss codification without seeming to pass judgement on the respective merits of codified and uncodified law. That controversy is one which I would rather avoid.

But it would be unreasonable to pass over codification without a word. For our purposes civil codes – which alone have any relevance – divide into three types. First of all, what may be called original codes,[22] that is where the attempt is made to codify (and modernise) the law existing in a particular territory, to think through the principles and rules which should inform the law. The Codes of France, Germany and Switzerland are particularly noteworthy here. Secondly, what one may call transplanted codes, when the codifying system borrows in whole or in large part a code already prepared for another system. Examples of this class are particularly numerous, and include the Civil Codes of Quebec, Holland, Japan and the Italian Code of 1865.[23] Thirdly, what may be termed Westernising codes, where a prime function of the code is to introduce European-style law into a developing country with the intention of 'modernising' society. Examples range from Turkey and Ethiopia to the Ivory Coast.[24] However interesting the second and third groups may be, it is the very small first group which alone raises the question whether private law and society can really be in step. The third type of code must, in the nature of things, contain many legal rules which are out of step with the society as it is; and we need not here deal with the difficulty experienced in having the legal rules accepted. And any divergences between law and society which are to be found in the first type are likely to be exaggerated in the second.

The preparation of an original code represents a unique opportunity to bring law into line with society at a single sweep; or at the very least to get rid of legal scaffolding.[25] Should codification generally be successful in these matters then we have a supreme irony for Savigny who opposed codification (at least for his own time in Germany) precisely because he saw uncodified law as the 'Spirit of the People'. Two issues are relevant. Can codification remove the significant divergence between law and society? Can it abolish legal scaffolding? Two points of time are important, namely the moment of codification and subsequently. These delicate questions must be mentioned, but a discussion of them would mean doubling the length of this volume without really affecting the basic thesis.[26]

Notes

1. We have been considering only Western or European law and, at that, not even codified law.
2. See already, Watson, *Legal Transplants*, pp. 95f.
3. *System des heutigen römischen Rechts* 1 (Berlin, Veit, 1840), especially pp. 1–65.
4. *Der Kampf um's Recht*, first published in 1872 (Vienna, Manz). The edition available to me was the twentieth (Vienna, Manz, 1921), p. 7; the translation is by P. A. Ashworth, *The Battle for Right* (London, Stevens, 1882), pp. 6f.
5. Jurists often express surprise at the small number of provisions in the French and German civil codes which have 'required' (i.e. undergone) change. The surprise is perhaps misplaced.
   I cannot agree with L. M. Friedman, 'Moreover, foolish traditions are tolerable as long as they are harmless': *History of American Law* (New York, Simon and Schuster, 1973), p. 19.
6. (Cambridge, Mass., Harvard University Press, 1936) translated by W. L. Moll.
7. *Sociology of Law*, p. 401.
8. See, with particular regard to labour law, O. Kahn-Freund, *Labour and the Law* (London, Stevens, 1972), pp. 2f. Recent research, moreover, has revealed a surprising ignorance of the legal rules even among the persons most affected; see B. Kutchinsky in *Knowledge and Opinion about Law* by A. Podgorecki *et al.* (London, Martin Robertson, 1973), pp. 101ff and the works he cites; H. L. A. Hart, *The Morality of the Criminal Law* (Jerusalem, Magnes Press, 1965), pp. 44f.
9. For a similar conclusion from a different angle see Watson, *Legal Transplants*, pp. 95f.
10. From his many writings it is enough to mention here *The Influence of Time and Place in Matters of Legislation*, chapter 4; *Truth v. Ashhurst*. The greater part of his concern was not with private law.
11. See, e.g. Dicey, *Law and Public Opinion*, especially pp. 126ff; Farrar, *Law Reform*, pp. 5ff.
12. With English law I have tried to give examples where the divergence outlived the reform movement directly inspired by Bentham.

13. For a summary of the modern movement for law reform see Farrar, *Law Reform*, pp. 1ff.
14. *Kampf*, pp. 8f; Ashworth's translation, p. 7.
15. 'The Path of the Law', *Harvard Law Review* 10 (1897), pp. 457ff, especially at p. 469.
16. *The Law of Contract*, 1st edit. (Oxford, Clarendon Press, 1961), p. vi.
17. Without any search I uncovered the following instances; T. E. Rogers, *The English Marriage-Laws and the Levitical Decrees* (London, Pickering, 1883); I.F., *Why May Not I Marry My Wife's Sister?* (London, SPCK, n.d.); C. Wordsworth, *On Marriage with a Deceased Wife's Sister* (London, Rivingtons, 1883); *Marriage with a Deceased Wife's Sister*, report of proceedings of a meeting in opposition to The Deceased Wife's Sister Bill held in Freemason's Hall, Lincoln's Inn Fields, on Thursday June 7, 1883, The Rt. Hon. Earl Beauchamp in the Chair (London, Church Printing Co., 1883); E. M. Shaw *Marriage as Affected by the Proposed Change in the Marriage Laws* (London, Rivingtons, 1883); G. Woollcombe, *Prohibitions in Marriage* (London, SPCK, n.d.); Lord Forbes, *Marriage with a Deceased Wife's Sister* (Aberdeen, Brown, 1883); J. Le Mesurier, *A Few Words on the Real Bearings of the Proposed Change in the Marriage Law* (Rivingtons, London, 1883); M. W. M. Dunn, *Is Marriage with a Deceased's Wife's Sister Lawful?* (London, Rivingtons, 1883); G. D. W. Ommanney, *Marriage with a Deceased Wife's Sister* (London, Parker, 1883); H. H. Duke, *The Question of Incest relatively to Marriage with Sisters in Succession*, 2nd edit. (London, Rivingtons, 1883) [1st edit. 1882]. There must be many more. One pamphlet in favour of the legislation talks of 'the appalling mass of pamphlet literature' on the subject: *Should Englishmen Be Permitted to Marry their Deceased Wives' Sisters?* by One Who Does Not Want To (London, Ridgway, 1883), p. 1.
18. Though he does not expressly restrict to modern society the idea of society in flux typically faster than the law in flux, Karl N. Llewellyn's discussion of the common points of departure for legal realism is particularly important: *Jurisprudence, Realism in Theory and Practice* (University of Chicago Press, 1962), p. 55.
19. See already Watson, *Legal Transplants*, pp. 95f.
20. This point will be developed in a forthcoming book provisionally entitled *The Nature of Law*.
21. See T. Hobbes, *Leviathan*, book 1, ch. 15 (especially from the eleventh law of nature onward).
22. See, e.g. R. Pound, 'Codification in Anglo-American Law' in *The Code Napoleon and the Common Law World*, edit. by B. Schwartz (New York, New York University Press, 1956), pp. 267ff at p. 278; Lawson, *Common Lawyer*, p. 49.
23. See, e.g. J. Limpens, 'Territorial Expansion of the Code', in *The Code Napoleon and the Common Law World*, pp. 92ff.

24. This classification leaves out of account codes which are prepared for conquered territories. These codes themselves, of which perhaps the most interesting are those made for India in the 19th century, can be arranged in various classes.
25. To avoid the possibility of misunderstanding it should be expressly stated that legal commentary and legal scaffolding are not the same thing.
26. From a vast literature let me cite F. F. Stone, 'A Primer on Codification', G. Trudel, 'The Usefulness of Codification: a Comparative Study of Quasi-Contract', A. Tunc, 'The Grand Outlines of the Code Napoleon', all in *Tulane Law Review* 29 (1954–55) respectively, at pp. 303ff, 311ff, 431; C. J. Morrow, 'An Approach to the Revision of the Louisiana Civil Code', *Louisiana Law Review* 19 (1949–50), pp. 59ff; 'Current Prospects for Revision of the Louisiana Civil Code', *Tulane Law Review* 33 (1958–59), pp. 143ff; L. J. de la Morandière, 'Preliminary Report of the Civil Code Reform Commission of France', *Louisiana Law Review* 16 (1955–56), pp. 1ff; H. R. Hahlo, 'Here lies the Common Law: Rest in Peace' (with comment by L. C. B. Gower), *MLR* 30 (1967), pp. 241ff; M. R. Topping & J. P. M. Vandenlinden, *'Ibi renascit ius commune'*, *MLR* 33 (1970), pp. 170ff; Mr. Justice Scarman, 'Codification and Judge-Made Law' (Lecture in the Faculty of Law, University of Birmingham, October 20, 1966); G. Marty & P. Raynaud, *Droit Civil 1, Introduction générale à l'étude du droit*, 2nd edit. (Paris, Sirey, 1972), pp. 127ff; H. & L. & J. Mazeaud, *Leçons de Droit Civil 1, Introduction à l'étude du droit*, 5th edit. by M. de Juglart (Paris, Montchrestien, 1972), pp. 61ff; the papers collected in *The Code Napoleon and the Common Law World* in particular, C. J. Friedrich, 'The Ideological and Philosophical Background', pp. 1ff; A. Tunc, 'The Grand Outlines of the Code', pp. 19ff; R. Pound, 'Codification in Anglo-American Law', pp. 267ff.

Chapter 12

STUDY OF LEGAL DEVELOPMENT

The conclusion that the relationship between legal rules and the society in which they operate is more tenuous than is usually supposed makes the questions of how, why and when legal developments occur more, not less, interesting and important. Each development seems to require a rather potent cause. If one were to investigate the causes of development one would find, I think, that no simple formula could be laid down, but each case had to be regarded individually. Yet one can, I believe, make a start on a systematic, rational study of the factors causing law to develop. In this final chapter I should like to suggest two possible approaches.

The first approach derives directly from the preceding chapters and scarcely needs setting down. I would like to suggest that a particular country be studied for a considerable period of its history during which it underwent marked changes in its circumstances whether social, economic, political or religious. One should then look at its private law to see how quickly, if at all, the legal rules did in general respond to the change in society. If one also looked at what are expressed as, or *ex facie* appear to be, the motives for the legal changes, and then related the apparent motives to the known changes in society, one would again have an insight into the real factors in legal development.

Secondly, in an earlier study I attempted to set out what I believed Comparative Law should be as an intellectual discipline in its own right.[1] It was, I suggested, a study of the relationship of one legal system and its rules with another. This relationship, I thought, was discoverable only by a study of the history of the system or of the rules, and that therefore Comparative Law was Legal History concerned with the relationship between systems.[2] But I suggested Comparative Law was also something more. In studying the similarities and differences between systems which have a relationship, one is better able to understand the particular factors which actually do shape and have shaped legal growth and change, and this, I hinted, may be the easiest approach to an appreciation of how law normally evolves. Hence, Comparative Law is also about the nature of law, especially about the nature of legal development, and is a branch of Jurisprudence.

The main type of relationships between systems arises because one borrowed from the other, or because both borrowed from a third. Since borrowing – often with modifications – is the main way in which the law of any Western system develops, at the centre of study of Comparative Law should be Legal Transplants.

In that work I accepted as true – as I still do – the impossibility of Comparative Law ever being completely systematic.³ But now I should like to set the scene – no more than that – for a more systematic treatment of the thesis with the help of the argument of the present work.⁴

Theoretically it should be possible to choose a legal subject which has common roots or at least one common root in several systems, and trace the factors which have influenced change. It should be possible to account for the legal details, existing or superseded, explaining why they are the same or why they differ in the systems, and why those persons who shape law have modified, abolished or kept unchanged the original rules. In addition, where the common root was grafted onto existing rules one should also be able to trace and explain the fate of these rules. Such a study should result, I think, in a better understanding of the factors which actually have influenced legal developments and, equally important, have prevented specific developments in particular jurisdictions. The particular qualities, values and attitudes prevalent in individual systems will also be highlighted.

From that theoretical position there will be a sad declension here. My hope, however, is to point the way. An instructive introductory area for study, I suggest, could be damage caused by animals within the systems which have been considerably influenced by the Roman *actio de pauperie*. Even with such a small topic there is material for a lifetime's study, and here I shall do nothing more than very briefly set out the law in South Africa, France, Austria, Germany and Louisiana, and call attention to a few peculiarities in development.

The point of departure is Roman law in the time of Justinian. It would be unreasonable here to look at earlier developments.

In the sixth century the owner of an animal which caused damage by acting contrary to nature – *contra naturam*, whatever that may mean – in circumstances where no man was responsible, was liable to pay the victim the amount of the damage or to surrender to him the wrong-doing animal.

For South Africa the main propositions were set out by De Villiers, C. J. in *South African Railways and Harbours* v. *Edwards*.⁵

(1) The *actio de pauperie* is in full force in South Africa. But the right to surrender the offending animal in lieu of paying damages – *noxae deditio* – is obsolete with us. (2) The action is based upon ownership. The English doctrine of *scienter* is not a portion of our law. (3) The action lies against the owner in respect of harm (*pauperies*) done by domesticated animals, such for instance as horses, mules, cattle, dogs, acting from inward excitement (*sponte feritate commota*). If the animal does damage from inward excitement or, as it is also called, from vice, it is said to act *contra naturam sui generis*; its behaviour is not considered such as is usual with a well-behaved animal of the kind. (4) On the other hand, if the act was not due to vice on the part of the animal but was provoked – in other words if there has been *concitatio*, the action does not lie. (5) Dating back as this form of remedy does to the most primitive times, the idea underlying the *actio de pauperie*, an idea which is still at the root of the action, was to render the owner liable only in cases where so to speak the fault lay with the animal. In other words for the owner to be liable, there must be something equivalent to *culpa* in the conduct of the animal. (6) Hence if the fault lies with the injured person himself he cannot recover, as he would have only himself to blame. If for instance he has provoked the animal, or has acted in such a way that the outburst could reasonably have been foreseen. (7) But stroking or petting a horse is not considered to be provocation (*concitatio*). If a horse kicks when petted, its behaviour is due to vice. The fault lies with the horse, not with the man who petted it, unless he had reason to know that the horse might kick. The learned Judge in the present case is of opinion that if the attentions of a person who stroked or petted a mule were met with a kick, such person would only have himself to blame for doing such a foolish thing. The kick, in the case of a mule, could have been foreseen. (8) Alfenus gives the following instance. A groom was leading a horse into a stable. The horse sniffed at a mare[6] which thereupon kicked the groom on the leg. The jurist holds that the action lies against the owner of the mare. In other words the incitement did not justify the mare in kicking. This case has been much debated. But whether Alfenus was right or wrong, in his view the solicitations of the horse were not considered to excuse the behaviour of the mare. She was said to have acted from innate perverseness. (9) The action does not lie if the animal was provoked by a third party, if for instance the animal was struck by a goad and kicks out. (10) Nor does the action lie if the injury was due to pure accident (*casus*); here nobody is con-

sidered to blame, as in *Cowell* v. *Friedman & Co.* (5 H.C.G. 22).

For France there is art. 1385 of the *Code Civil*:

Le propriétaire d'un animal ou celui qui s'en sert, pendant qu'il est à son usage, est responsable du dommage que l'animal a causé, soit que l'animal fût sous sa garde, soit qu'il fût égaré ou échappé.[7]

For Austria, §1320 of the *Allgemeines bürgerliches Gesetzbuch*:

Wird jemand durch ein Tier beschädigt, so ist derjenige dafür verantwortlich, der es dazu angetrieben, gereizt oder zu verwahren vernachlässigt hat. Derjenige, der das Tier hält, ist verantwortlich, wenn er nicht beweist, daß er für die erforderliche Verwahrung oder Beaufsichtigung gesorgt hat.[8]

For Germany, §833 of the *Bürgerliches Gesetzbuch*:

Wird durch ein Tier ein Mensch getötet oder der Körper oder die Gesundheit eines Menschen verletzt oder eine Sache beschädigt, so ist derjenige, welcher das Tier hält, verpflichet, dem Verletzten den daraus entstehenden Schaden zu ersetzen. Die Ersatzpflicht tritt nicht ein, wenn der Schaden durch ein Haustier verursacht wird, das dem Berufe, der Erwerbstätigkeit oder dem Unterhalte des Tierhalters zu dienen bestimmt ist, und entweder der Tierhalter bei der Beaufsichtigung des Tieres die im Verkehr erforderliche Sorgfalt beobachtet oder der Schaden auch bei Anwendung dieser Sorgfalt entstanden sein würde.[9]

And for Louisiana, art. 2321 of the *Civil Code*:

The owner of an animal is answerable for the damage he has caused; but if the animal had been lost, or had strayed more than a day, he may discharge himself from this responsibility, by abandoning him to the person who has sustained the injury; except where the master has turned loose a dangerous or noxious animal, for then he must pay for all the harm done, without being allowed to make the abandonment.

Merely to set out these provisions is to pose the major questions. By what steps and for what reasons did these systems with the sole exception of South Africa eliminate any need for the animal to be acting *contra naturam* before there is liability? And how and why has *contra naturam* come in South Africa – and, indeed, in Europe much before – to be *contra naturam sui generis*? Surrender of the offending animal has disappeared from all these jurisdictions named except for Louisiana where it survives in a modified form. Why?

Germany – but of these jurisdictions only Germany, and Germany only from 1908 – draws a distinction between animals in general and domestic animals kept to serve the business, occupation or livelihood of the owner. How has this come about? The German, French and Louisianan Codes seem – on the face of it, though the reality may be different – to make the owner of the animal liable automatically for any injury it causes. Liability under the French provision was in fact at first thought to be based on presumed fault on the part of the person in charge of the animal. The Austrian Code, on the other hand, begins by making liable the person who incited the animal to the injury, excited it or neglected to take the proper precautions in respect of it. What is the real meaning and explanation of difference here? Of the five modern systems, the uncodified law of South African is very much closer to the Roman rules than are any of the Codes. Yet South African law, in sharp distinction to that of Austria, France or Germany, is a 'Mixed System', that is one of the systems which have developed under the strong influence of both Roman and English law.

Every time a change is deliberately made a choice has been exercised. Often the retention of a legal rule is also the result of choice. To isolate the factors in the choices which are made is to go a long way towards understanding how law develops and also how law is in fact related to its society. In the present context it is possible even at the outset to list some factors which might have been influential for development: attitudes towards animals or to kinds of animals; theories on the nature of animals and their capacity for rational thought; ideas of moral responsibility whether for an individual's acts or for his keeping a potentially dangerous thing, or simply ideas on the duties imposed by ownership; theories of causation; social and economic conditions in the area in question; particularly striking episodes; and the authority of individual legal thinkers. Yet the lesson of the preceding chapters is precisely that in explaining legal development the isolation of factors such as those just listed is in general not enough. That can tell us why the particular development occurred, and not some other; but it does not explain why development occurred at all, or at that precise time. For that we must search for the impetus which was strong enough to overcome the law's inertia.

Finally, let me mention one further legal problem. In very many modern Civil Law Systems it is a criminal offence to abstain from coming to the aid of a person in grave danger when that aid can be rendered without exposing oneself to serious danger. Again when of his own volition someone intervenes to protect the person or property of another, and suffers physical injury or death he or his representatives has a civil action for compensation against the person he was helping. The first of these propositions seems to have taken its modern form in the second half of the nineteenth century, and the second is rather later still. The precise scope of these two propositions naturally varies considerably from country to country, and there has been a great deal of legal borrowing. It would seem that in the development of these propositions the very different Roman concept of *negotiorum gestio* – which was received in Civil Law systems – played an important role. For the Romans, a person who, without authorisation, reasonably and with useful effect intervened to save another's property from damage had right to the *actio negotiorum gestorum* (for not more than the benefit he had imposed) to recover financial loss which he thereby suffered. An examination of the factors, social, economic and otherwise, causing the modern developments in some but not all of the Civil Law systems would, I believe, be very revealing. The topic gains in interest when we notice that in general in Anglo-American law it is no crime to refrain from aiding a person in great danger even when no risk would be involved in rendering aid; and that to suffer physical injury when aiding another person does not, of itself, give right to an action for compensation from the person aided. Anglo-American law has in general not accepted any doctrine comparable to that of the Roman *negotiorum gestio*. Could it be that the main reason for the fundamental difference between modern Civil Law systems and Anglo-American law as regards the two propositions is not to be found in varying social, economic and political factors, but in the cast of thought of their lawyers which in turn would depend on whether or not *negotiorum gestio* had been received? If so, what would one make of the fact that Scots law, when very open to the influence of Roman law, received *negotiorum gestio* (which still flourishes), but is now much influenced by English law and has never accepted the two propositions?[10]

Notes

1. *Legal Transplants*. The remainder of this chapter originally formed the starting point of a lecture delivered at the University of California at Berkeley in December 1974.
2. *Legal Transplants*, p. 6.
3. See already F. H. Lawson in the preface to his edition of W. W. Buckland and A. D. McNair, *Roman Law and Common Law* (Cambridge, 1952), p. xii.

4. To my utter astonishment my discussion of the scope of an academic discipline of comparative law (especially at pp. 4f) has led to the belief that I was excluding social variables from the factors causing law to develop, though (it is said) societal factors creep back: review of *Legal Transplants* by R. B. Seidman, *Boston University Law Review* 1975, pp. 682ff. I should like to stress that I have never intended to exclude social factors from the causes of development. Some of the difficulties experienced by the reviewer would seem to result from his lack of the relevant historical knowledge.

5. 1930 AD 3 at pp. 9f.

6. Actually in the case considered by Alfenus the animal sniffed at was a female mule.

7. 'The owner of an animal or the person who uses it, while it is subject to his use, is responsible for the loss which the animal has caused, whether the animal was under his care or had wandered off or had escaped.'

8. 'If anyone is injured by an animal, then that person is responsible who incited it, excited it or neglected to guard it. The person who keeps the animal is responsible if he does not prove that he provided for the necessary guarding or superintendence.'

9. 'If by an animal a human is killed or the health of a human is injured, or a thing is damaged, then the person who keeps the animal is obliged to make good the resultant loss to the injured person. The duty of compensation does not arise if the injury is caused by a domestic animal which is intended to serve the profession, the earning capacity or the upkeep of the keeper of the animal, and either the keeper of the animal in superintending the animal showed the care appropriate to the business or the loss would have occurred even if that care had been shown.'

10. The best starting point for an investigation into the two propositions is in the papers in *The Good Samaritan and the Law* edit. by J. M. Ratcliffe (Garden City, N.Y., Anchor Books, 1966).

Index

actio Publiciana 33
Agrippina 38, 116
Allen, C. K. 95
Allgemeines bürgerliches Gesetzbuch 143
ancient demesne 54
animals 82f, 141ff
Archer's Case 51f
Atiyah, P. S. 133
Augustus 123f

barter 18f
Barton, J. 46n.42, 60n.30
Beinart, B. 81
'benefit of clergy' 92ff
Bentham, J. 132
bigamus 93
Blackstone, W. 47f, 104f
Bohannan, P. 7
Bugnyon, P. 81
burgage 53f

California 108ff
Carr, F. 63f
Carter-Ruck, P. F. 61, 71f
Cassidy v. *Daily Mirror* 65f
Chambliss, W. 62
Cherokees 2
Cheshire, G. C. 48f, 54ff
Chudleigh's Case 51
Civil code (Louisiana) 143
Claudius 38ff, 116, 135
Code (of Justinian) 24f
Code civil 143
codification 136f
communauté 106ff
condictio 17f
Constans 39
Constantius 39
'constructive malice aforethought' 94
Cooper, Lord 1
copyhold 54ff
criminal law 77ff
Cromwell, O. 49, 57

Daube, D. 26ff, 123
defamation 61ff
Defamation Act, 1952 66, 68, 71
depositum 15ff
De Villiers, C. J. 141f

Devlin, Lord 79
Diamond, A. S. 2
Dicey, A. V. 119, 128n. 32
Digest 18f, 35f
Dionysius of Halicarnassus 23f, 26f
direct representation 20, 105
divine services 50

Ehrlich, E. 131
emancipatio 24f
Engels, F. 3f, 6ff, 121
error 20
Esher, Lord 70

'fair comment' 70, 92
Faulks Committee 61f, 64f, 70
felony 77f
frankalmoign 50
French law 99
Friedman, L. M. 11n.21
furtum manifestum 34ff
furtum nec manifestum 34ff

Gaius 18, 23, 26, 35, 38f, 41f
gavelkind 53
gentiles 40
Gower, L. C. B. 62, 120f, 125
Groenewegen, S. van 80f

Heever, Van den, J. A. 101f
Henry VIII 51, 56, 91f, 116, 121, 135
Hexabiblos 84
Holmes, O. W. 79
Hulton v. *Jones* 65
Hunter, Lord 112n. 30

Ihering, R. von 2, 8, 131
incest 37ff
inertia 8, 115ff
insurance 105f

Justin I 116

Kahn-Freud, O. 100, 106ff, 110
Kleffens, E. N. van 1
knight service 50ff
Koschaker, P. 99

larceny 79
Laurie, R. B. 104

Lawson, F. H. 48, 58
legacy 41
lex Poetilia 117
libel 61ff
literal contract 13f

Maine, H. 2
Maitland, F. W. 49
mancipatio 15, 31ff
mandatum 16f
Marx, K. (and Marxists) 3f, 6ff, 91, 94
Megarry, R. E. 49
misdemeanour 77f
Montesquieu 1
mutuum 17f

negotiorum gestio 145
nexum 117f
novation 41f
noxal surrender 41f

O'Callaghan v. *Chaplin* 82f

Pahad v. *Director of Food Supplies* 100f
partnership 20
patria potestas 23ff, 122ff
Paul 14, 18f, 36
peculium 24ff, 122ff
Plato Films v. *Speidel* 69f, 117
Plautus 35
Porter Committee 64ff, 71, 117
Pound, R. 2f, 44, 83, 89
Pringsheim, F. 2
Proculians 19

Quia Emptores 50, 80

R. v. *Dent* 79
registration of title 55ff, 120
Reid, J. P. 2
remainders 51f
res mancipi 31ff
res nec mancipi 31ff
'rolled-up plea' 71, 92
Romulus 23f
Ruoff, T. B. F. 57

S. v. *Attawari* 95f, 97n.24
Sabinians 19

Sachers, E. 26
sale 14f, 18f, 87f, 99ff
Saskatchewan 105f
Savigny, F. von 1, 6, 8, 48, 121
Sawer, G. 1
scaffolding 87ff
Scarman, L. 119
Schulz, F. 46n.48
Scott v. *Sampson* 68, 70
Scottish Law Commission 102f, 121, 136
senatusconsultum Macedonianum 117
Sergeanty 50, 52f
Servius 42
slander 61ff
Smith, T. B. 102, 112n.25
socage 50, 53, 55
Social Engineering 2f, 83, 89, 91
South African Railways v. *Edwards* 141f
Spider's Web 66
Stair, Lord 16
Statute of Frauds 80
Statute of Uses 51, 80, 91f, 116, 121, 135
Statute of Wills 51, 92
stipulatio 12ff, 17f, 41f, 87f
subordinate legislation 95
succession 40f
Sutherland, R. 103

traditio 88f
transplants 98ff
treason 77f
Tumanov 4
Twelve Tables 12, 16, 24f, 34f, 40, 82, 88f

Ulpian 36, 88
use 90ff

vagrancy statutes 62
Visigoths 107f
Volksgeist 1, 130

Wade, E. C. S. 61
Wade, H. W. R. 49
Wilkinson, A. B. 103
Williams, J. 49
Windscheid, B. 83f.